June 2010

To Cindy and John,
Thanks for the shelter!
Enjoy!!

STONE WHISPERER

P·O·E·M·S

Hendrik D. Gideonse

**THE GANDALF PRESS
BROOKLIN, MAINE**

THE GANDALF PRESS
119 Old County Road
Brooklin, ME 04616

Copyright © 2010 by Hendrik D. Gideonse

First edition, February, 2010
Second edition, February, 2010
Third edition, March, 2010

All rights reserved, including the right to reproduce this book or portions thereof in any form whatsoever.

The Gandalf Press Speakers Bureau can bring the author to your live event. For more information, contact The Gandalf Press Speakers Bureau at 1-207-359-8510.

ISBN 978-0-557-27575-5

For Judi K. Beach,
poet of substance, mentor, and friend
whose steely insistence at the end
bade me transcribe my tunes
and sing them for *my* friends

Poems in this volume previously published elsewhere include:

"Red Suspenders and *Wild Horses*" in the Weekly Packet (Blue Hill, ME) and a privately published memorial volume for Joel White

"Waylaid" in the Ellsworth American

"April After Ice: Augusta to Belfast," "Seasons Juxtaposed," "Porpoises," "An Existential Moment Slow to Come," "MLK Jr.," "Hands," "Tendrils," "An Electric Blanket Gone South," and "Dmitri's" in Eggemoggin Reach Review, Volumes I and II

"70" in the Classbook for the Amherst 1958 50th Reunion

"Savoring First Conversations" in the Bangor Daily News

Table of Contents

Introduction...1

Insight
    Stone Whisperer...7
    Mother's Hands...9
    Enigma...12
    Porpoises...13
    Lupine...15
    Tattoo...16
    Fool's Gold...18
    Allure...21
    Prophecy (Here I Am. Are Your Lips Pursed?)...23
    Hogan's Haiku...25
    Mantra...28
    St. Lô...29
    Ashes and Hope...30
    To Balzac and Ray Carver...33

Sight
    Signals...37
    Variations on a Theme: Axial Shift; the Spin to
            Spring...39
    On a Twisted Sledge Norwottuck's Called to Rest...40
    Cemetery...41
    Pigeons...43
    Quiver...45
    Dmitri's...47
    A Goldfinch and Edouard - September 2, 1996...48
    Confirmation...50
    Seasons Juxtaposed...52
    A Reading...54

Hands...56
How Much More Do You Need to Know?...59
Time...61
Fisher...67
Grief's Bad Penny...68
Thanksgiving Gift, 2000...70
Symmetry...74

Action
Her Voice Is Not Stilled...77
Glow...79
Love Abuilding...82
Ralph...84
Where Will It End?...86
Faithful to the Core...88
In Praise of Small Packages...90
Mycelium: My Town...91
Waylaid...92
Loving Tracks...95
Still Type A...96
There Are Others...98

Patience
Telltales...105
An Existential Moment Slow to Come...106
Haiku for a Truncated Spring...108
Puzzles...109
Of Maple Syrup and Dandelions Gone to Seed...114
Respiration...115
Mid January, the Coast of Maine...116

Contemplation
    Tendrils...121
    MLK, Jr....125
    Red Suspenders and *Wild Horses*...127
    Unheeded Meaning...130
    Spencer William's Hard Lovely Morn...132
    70...136
    Remembrance...138
    Come Spring......140
    Lost Dog, Almost Gone...142
    Cat's Cradle...146
    April After Ice: Augusta to Belfast...148

Rapture
    Savoring First Conversations...153
    First Kisses...154
    Lucky Dog...156
    Mellow...159
    Pancake...162
    Dandelion Seed Puffs...164
    First Fruit...165
    Glowworms...166
    Vacation...167
    Passing Storm...169
    Were I Solomon, This Would Be One of My Songs...170
    An Electric Blanket Gone South...172

Appendix: Eggemoggin Writers' Collaborative Prospectus...175

Colophon...180

Introduction

You are holding in your hands a volume never intended.

Not, that is, until just a very few months ago. Last spring, in this latest multi-year adventure in writing, one completely different from the ones of the forty years preceding, I realized I had a substantial number of poems worth bringing together in some sort of milestone of my progress.

And then I was invited to a workshop in Camden where I was first exposed to the incredible advances in technology which make it possible to lay out and produce professional volumes and do so most economically. A few months later a member of the Deer Isle Writers Group read from the Lulu book her husband prepared for her from her novel. A seed was planted.

For me, poetry is a form of autobiography. I like to address every-day matters – family, surroundings, affinities, love, work and service, grief and pain, play – while fully recognizing that 'every day' doesn't necessarily mean 'simple.' I try to illuminate, exclaim, underscore, offer a lens, and eschew "guess-what's-behind-the-sheet-by-the-way-it's-draped-over-the-object-it-covers." The concept of verisimilitude is a continuing challenge for me: can I, as close as I can tell, generate in a reader a feeling/reaction/understanding nearly identical to the one which suffused me and made me want to share?

I never thought writing poetry was easy, but I have come to appreciate how much it entails taking risks. Will the achievement, the outcome, ever match my intention? And what about the reactions and assessments of others? While we poets may be our own severest critics, the assessments of *others* probably hold the greatest potential for personal discomfort or embarrassment. But they are also the source of one's greatest help and support. It needs saying, therefore, that every poem here has been exposed to the eyes and ears of others in quite formal collaborative reviews, often repeatedly and periodically over a decade as my voice as a poet has come to be more clearly defined.

As noted, self-judgments as well as those of one's colleagues are the stimuli to the enhancement of one's own craft. When a writer is in the presence of a group of individuals genuinely committed to their own mutual growth and improvement, the benefit can be just enormous. Conversely, when criticism is delivered absent a commitment to care or generosity, or, worse, becomes tied to egotism or a penchant for theater, the consequences for a writer can be disconcerting if not devastating.

My own growth is so intimately connected to the mutual support I have received from my colleagues on Deer Isle and the Blue Hill Peninsula I have to acknowledge here the huge role they have played, and special mention within the larger group must be given, in addition to Judi, to Anne Larkosh Burton, Maureen Farr, Brenda Gilchrist, Nancy Hodermarsky, Mickey Jacoba, Deborah Wedgwood Marshall, and Norma Voorhees Sheard.

In this volume every poem begins with a generally brief boxed introduction formatted and placed in a way which allows the readers to pass over it easily if they wish. As I began to read aloud before strangers at open mikes and poetry gatherings I found myself saying a few words of introduction for each of my poems. And, over time, feedback has made it clear the introductions were appreciated and contributed to listener understanding and access. If live audiences found it helpful, I thought I could employ the concept here.

Lastly, a word about how the poems were organized for this volume. Several years ago Pat Ranzoni and I were invited to the Unitarian Universalist Church in Ellsworth, ME, for a poetry night. The organization for the evening was quite informal; the two of us could play it any way we wanted. She and I conferred for a few minutes. We decided that one of us would start with a poem and then the other would respond with another. Over the evening what happened was a kind of conversation through alternating poems between two poets that left both of us and the audience genuinely intrigued. Maybe it was a totally one-off experience, but it made such an impression on me that in this volume I've tried to create a conversation with myself on the half dozen themes. I leave it to you, the reader, to judge its viability.

Hendrik D. Gideonse

INSIGHT

> *Balancing stones is a relatively new pastime for me, yet it has been an ever-present, quasi-meditative endeavor for more than a decade. I had done it, large stones and small, over and over, on islands and beaches and quarries all over the coast of Maine. From time to time I had helped others learn to do it as well, but it took a brief conversation with a stranger to make me really think about it.*

Stone Whisperer

"Has anyone ever called you a stone whisperer," she asked him,
Riding the ferry from Vinalhaven to the mainland.
She'd seen him whiling time away
At Grimes Park waiting for the boat to load,
And in the chill breeze returning she asked him
How he'd balanced all those hefty, jagged rocks
On their narrowest points,
To stand however briefly as silent sentinels on crag and
      ledge,
Full of stored energy subject to release by a breath of wind,
The brush of a herring gull's wing,
Or the slight weight of a squirrel bent upon a stand to shred a
      cone.

He told her he didn't whisper; he listened —
Listened to the many voices in each stone,

Listened with his hands, as nearly balanced stones
Talked to him through his fingertips
Telling him just where their centers lay,

Listened with his ears, as the subtle sounds of scratch and
      lock
Told him where the stone's point lay aligned
From its centered mass to that of the earth itself,

And, finally, listened to the murmurs in his back

Warning him, for his own comfort,
It was time to stop, to try again another day
To once more find the voices hidden in the hearts of stones.

> *My parents were tough acts to follow. When they both passed away within three weeks of each other it took me pages and pages to memorialize them, but that was years before I got serious about poetry. I found writing about my father much easier than writing about my mother. But that's because my relationship to her was much more complicated than to him. One day a friend asked me how, given my academic, administrative, and policy career, I'd ever found myself an avocational builder. I told him the little story built into the middle of this poem, and everything else just fell in place.*

Mother's Hands

Mother's hands were rarely idle.

They hooked rugs,
Molded figurines for a Christmas creche,
Painted watercolors and oils.

They knit, crocheted,
Performed ballets with the spindles
Splayed out before the lace making wheel.
Her fingers replaced fuses,
Castled kings, dealt out hands of solitaire,
Turned novels' pages,
Played the upright in the den.
She wallpapered all the upstairs rooms,
Adorned wooden boxes,
Made dolls, repaired furniture,
Planted gardens.
She wrapped saved string on progressively larger balls,
Decorated birthday cakes,
Cut celery and carrots for supper.
Now and again her fingers searched through a thousand
 buttons for just the right one
In a box that still waits patiently

Twenty years after her death should she need it once again.
She signed checks and report cards,
Wrote letters to camp and college,
And one year early in my life filled out my application
To Saturday shop class at Kensington School.

She thought I might like it, she'd said.

And, oh, it turned out, I did!

Mother dutifully pressed a rough-hewn, painted tray into tea
    service.
Dad used a revolving tie rack to store the ones
He'd long ago retired from service.
(The hammered copper ash trays,
On the other hand, he'd used a lot!)
These were the bare beginnings
That reached full flower four years after Mother passed
When, in an acre hole in Maine's woods,
I began a twenty-year binge of building –

First a summer house for my family,
Then later a winter one for me.
Almost annually thereafter new spaces grew for boats and
    files,
For a Harley and a truck,
A cabin for my goddaughter and her partner,
Space for writing, for tools, wood, and other big-boy toys,
Then a place to sweat,
And still another to sup, sing, gather, and dance.

Before Mother died she saw a photo of a houseboat her
    grandsons and I had built.
She recalled the Saturday morning shop class she'd sent me
    to,

And then revealed to me, thirty-six years later,
A more freighted though unstated reason
That had accompanied the "something you might like to do."
She told me that even though just nine, she'd known
I'd someday marry and have a family of my own;
"You'll *never*," she had vowed, "be as incompetent with tools
    as your father!"

My mother's hands were rarely idle, yes,
And her intention, in retrospect, no less pointed
Than tools they'd once held,
Though long shielded by a scabbard it may have been.

> *The passage of years has leeched out the discomfort, though the image remains a haunting one.*

Enigma

She stands,
Still,
Unclothed,
Left hand to the jamb,
The casement window
Open to the snowy morning
Laid out before her.

The sash gapes just wide enough
For her to cast out seeds to feed
The doves and jays and smaller birds
Whose lives she courts and cultivates
With barely well-concealed intensity.

Cold air spills across the sill
And down her knees and toes.
She leans,
Vulnerable,
Alone,
Riding the crest of a wave
Of quiet self-deceit,
The still moment
Veiling murmurs
Of tumult and terror deep inside.

> *When a deeply rooted and long held belief is suddenly rendered inadequate.*

Porpoises

I first saw porpoises in Long Island Sound,
Long lines of them, parallel to the shore,
Headed west or east at Old Field Beach.
Then later in Eggemoggin Reach
I'd see them from my boat on certain days
When wind was light and water not too broken,
Their glistening backs and dorsal fins
Would slowly break the surface.
They'd breathe, and wheel beneath
To break again some fifty feet away
In what directions no one could safely say.

One time, in irons and barely rising on small swells,
A mother and her child played all around my stern,
Her "poosh," its "pish," each breathing
On their easy broaches left and right,
To underscore the image held so long,
Of porpoise gentle, sure, together, pure.

And then late last fall in empty Center Harbor
Standing at the floatless pier I was amazed to see,
In spaces I never imagined them to be, a dozen of them,
    perhaps,
Playing out the chilly setting sun at highest tide,
The gentle arcs of pairs and threes
Turning slowly here and there,
A twist, a roll, a tag team match at watery play,
Until in the upper corner of my eye
A dorsal fin exploded up
To streak straight as an arrow

Seventy yards or more, unerring,
To a spot just near where my boat
Would have floated had she not been
In her winter shed,
And in that singular and swift event
Augment the images of gentleness and play
With proof of brutish power and violent intent.

> *What one sees is not necessarily what is there.*

Lupine

Electric blue, flecked gold, her eyes,
Framed by an auburn mane brushed wild,
Shift skittishly around her space,
To guard, cover, and protect
And always serve to lead away
Any who might get close.

Wild, yet still not free,
Haunted by her genes
And demons of the hunt,
And stories from the past
That hang nooselike
Around the neck of a future
Dreamed but not to be,
Her past is feral but yet a prison,
And like the ancient Spartan lad
Whose false sense of pride -- or shame --
Makes him hide the fox beneath his robe,
She is devoured
From the inside out.

> *This might just as easily have been titled((if somewhat awkwardly)* 'Regeneration: Time on the Water Doing What It's Supposed To.'

Tattoo

The captured leisure of a time long gone by –
'Swinging on the Gate' –
Plays softly on NPR.
Nearly equivalent breezes
Dust my arms and face
Reclining here afloat on
October's leaf-speckled Oxford, Ohio, waters,
On the deck of a houseboat built
Ten years before in play
But with a serious purpose of teaching sons to
Design,
Measure,
Measure,
Then cut.

Another summer tails into autumn
(Possible frost tomorrow night,
Certain storm later after the witching hour!);
It seems impossible
Given the balm about us.
This peacefulness spawns memories –
Strawberry daiquiries fashioned
By the north country Valkyrie
Whose deftly captured –
And then painstakingly executed –
Irises and sunflowers
I now wear proudly
Where my sleeves might be

Had I had any on.
Who'd have thought Brooklin
Would ever have so gotten under my skin?

> *The first, and at that time presumed to be final, version of this was written before a sustained encounter painfully unraveled. Only after it was long, long over did it become clear that what had seemed evidence of promise should have been seen as a warning of impending disaster. Changing less than a half dozen words was all it took.*

Fool's Gold

Unbroken mats of
Rock-wool batts of cloud
Have threatened all this day
To drop and smother
All which lies beneath.

Late in the day
A narrow strip
Opens to the west,
A leading edge of cloud,
A certain brightness,
Glinting, indirect,
A glow above, behind,
Although a wisp or two
Before the leading edge
Shine bright reflected
Whitened gold.

The leading edge grows,
Bolder,
Golder,
To birth a burning orange disk of sun
Dropping fast to fill the gap
And then just as fast is gone.

But in that moment
It was there
The stage I'm on
Is briefly bathed
In orange flood
That starkly strikes
Each tree and window,
Shutter, door, and flag,
Trans-tinting them
By briefest splash
Of molten light.

And just as fast
The orange world,
That briefly was
Returns to gray.

The swiftly fallen star
Sends its regrets
Exchanging fire
For softer energies
Of reflected light.

First pink,
To skim the rolling tips
Of waves of under-clouds,
Then moister, fatter swells of rouge
That grow to purples,
Mauves, magentas,
Exhausting Ms. Chicago's
Party palette,
A heat and fire
And passionate intensity,
A dozen minutes

Of November sunset,
Fair warning
After summer's long
And opening act.

> *Affairs of the heart can be unpredictable. And despite Yogi Berra's admonition, sometimes they're not over even when they are over. Herewith a miller moth acting out.*

Allure

I spend my days spread wide
Tucked in some crevice flat,
No profile from the side,
Unless I'm viewed from straight above.
But when the dark has come
I search out points of light
Growing brighter bit by bit,
And borne on large thin wings,
Erratic though my flight might seem,
Each zig or zag I make
Successively approximates
The source of beacons
To give me light
Or give me death.

In deepening dark
A man and son kneel talking
Quietly head to head
Before a sliding damper door.
The softwood kindling's more than caught,
And firmly implicates the birch
And maple splits lain just above;
The fire inside grows fierce.
Their words touch grief and loss,
The added pain of letting go.

I watch their talk,
Bounce off the glowing white
Of their shirts,

Flit back and forth across
The damper's close-spaced slots,
And fly straight in upon the fire
Consumed with neither sound nor flash,
Assured that as the
Million more such flames
Relight themselves
In timeless flow,
My instant resurrection
Swings a green lamp
For an endless train
Of rampant immolations.

> *I'd met her 30 months before; she "lit up my scoreboard" but that time turned out not to be quite right for her. And then a second chance emerged and notes I'd taken at the time of the first encounter for a poem for her I thought I'd try but never did, suddenly seemed worth working on, a little like a piece of clothing given to you as a youth you'd finally grown into. The title and last stanza are drawn directly from part of her story as told to me when first we met.*

Prophecy (Here I Am! Are Your Lips Pursed?)

The mushroom cap of my headlights
Rode on and on before the ever-lengthening stalk
Of the new black macadam roadway taking me home;
Broken yellow in the middle sometimes punctuated the
Solid white lines on either side.

George Harrison filled my car.
Singing what was on my mind –
Will my love grow, will it show,
I don't want to leave her now –
But I did.

The yellow lines seemed to say on-again off-again,
But suddenly they became solid,
Lined up side by side but never touching,
Charting a path beyond my capacity to see and believe.

I like my time alone
In what Hogan clearly thinks of as his rolling cave,
But I craved time alone with her, too,
Active time talking,
Quiet time, just listening to something,
Time to touch,
Time building shared memories.
She wanted to take it slow,

And while I thought I had energy and feeling in reserve,
That my heart was clear and
My patience infinite,
It was not to be that time.

Here I am thirty months later,
Walking back and forth at the website
Where I found her a second time,
And I swear I could hear her whistle!

> *In retrospect . . . I should have paid far more attention to my third stanza, where the real prophecy lay. The poem works, I think, so far as rekindled hope goes. After barely more than thirty days of that second deep mutual attraction, though, the hope was dashed, now nearly incapable of being recalled save for this poem. The month of intense exploration revealed, tant pis, far more there than met the eye; a future would have been far too strenuous. I backed up and broke it off. Days later a revised on-line profile declared her heart broken over a high-hope candidate being 'scared' by her directness and further cautioned future prospects 'no overly sensitive poets need apply.'*
>
> *Oh, well . . . .*

> *In the spring of 2006, Anne Burton, a writer colleague with whom I love to banter and zing e-mailed me a baker's dozen plus one haiku written by cats asking whether I thought my dog "could do as well." I talked with Hogan; no surprise, he immediately rose to the challenge generating one for every haiku syllable . . .*

Hogan's Haiku

I *heard* your whistle!
I'll bring you your damn ball; just
give me leave to pee!

Yeah, I'm a dog, but
sometimes I *like* to trot, each
side's legs in tandem.

Of *course* I am proud!
I caught your ball despite its
incompetent bounce!

Smart? You got it! I
run to *get* the ball; there's no
need to run it *back*.

Most of the time I
have the patience of Job but
one more treat, hunh, hunh?

Quimby* makes messes!
His tail's a scallop drag for
leaves, grass, mud, and twigs.

*Before Hogan, my favorite playmate and a frequent visitor thereafter!

Don't look at *me*, boss.
If Quim had wanted all his
food *he'd* have eaten it.

Yeah, right, if I could!
You try to tuck a stump like
mine between your legs.

Ball, bone, ring, or toy?
The two-pawed pounce says to me
each is still a mouse!

Me? *Me?* I didn't
do *any*thing. The wrapper
shreds lie like a rug.

Don't poke me. It's my
right to encroach you to the
far edge of the bed.

Those teeth marks on the
cutting board? Hell, the lamb soaked
into the wood, boss!

Keeping the tile floor
tongue-clean all around the stove?
No charge, boss, no charge.

Look, I stand or sit
on your feet to keep your hand
where it can pet me.

Besides, if you'd trim
my nails, good sir, they wouldn't
hurt your feet so much.

My nightly licking
of your legs says I forgive
your imperfections.

My boss is truly
odd, though. Anne sends catterel,
he channels my dogg . . .

> *As one ages sometimes tiny events, savored over time, assume increasing importance in the constellation of one's life. For a person like me from a family like mine, language is almost sacred, so when it fails I've always known to take careful notice.*

Mantra

Sitting across a tiny table
In a small store that
Sixteen years later would
Disappear in the cataclysm of Mount St. Helen,
This gorgeous young earth mother
Leaking libido before my very eyes
(Part of me doing my best
To soak every bit of it up),
Listened as I tried to explain
In increasingly halting terms
How the loss of Bobby the month before
Made me feel
Despair, powerless, undone.
I came to a complete halt,
Tears flowing down my face.
She paused before my silence,
Laid her hands on mine, and said
Slowly, gently, never-to-be-forgotten
"If words don't make it . . .
Then don't make it words."

> *Honor, reverence, acknowledgment, connection all in a flash.*

St. Lô
    (July, 1944)

The license plate electrified me –
Disabled veteran, "ST LO."
The vehicle pulled to the gas pump;
I could see the driver preparing to get out.
I eased into place along side his rear bumper,
The license plate burning into me,
A message brimming to come out.
I awaited his appearance and then waited some more.
Finally he emerged from his vehicle.
I stuck my head out the window saying
"I presume from your plate that you were there?"
A large man, his grizzled face looked puzzled
As he walked over to me.
Noticing a hearing aid,
I repeated more firmly what I had just said.
"Yes," he said, "I was there.
I was one of the lucky ones who came back."
"Sir," I said, "all I wanted to say is 'Thank you!'
I want you to know how much I appreciate your service to
       us."
"I spent my 21st birthday in England," he said,
"So many were left behind," his eyes welling up.
I said 'I understand' but I was in error;
I really should have said 'I know'
(His ready tears after sixty-five years
Gave me the clue I hadn't had a moment before).
His face leaned toward mine,
His hand reached toward me;
I clasped it. "Thank *you*," he said.

> *This chronicles events from the 'last century,' but the young man is now twenty-one and his mother remains at least as angry a person now as she was then; I am probably one of the very few poets in the world licensed and trained to carry. Through the continuing subsequent trauma, the picture of him and me taken by his eventual adoptive parents still occupies a treasured place on my mantle.*

Ashes and Hope

He was a small boy, not yet ten,
But going on thirty-five.
He brought me flowers,
A tulip first, then nasturtiums,
And, after, little carrots and turnips.

He spent as much time watching
My new pond grow from
A clay slip puddle as did I,
His eyes and, later, hands
Intent upon holding close the mysteries
Of eggs to tadpoles to frogs,
First brown, then green, then leopard.
He caught them, as most boys do,
But his moves were painstakingly slow
And he held his temporary captives
With a gentleness surprisingly sure and sweet.

Every day, only rarely every other, from mid-spring
To fall he came to visit, so serious, so reserved.
He'd watch, ask about tools and techniques.
One rainy day, his black and red Wellingtons doffed,
He entertained himself at computer solitaire.
And the day I inadvertently made him giggle was an
      unintended triumph,

A rare glimpse of child in all that seriousness.
("Oh, I put my flower money away for college," he would
 say to me,
Unaware there are many ways to meet such needs,
That doing well in school *now* is the better investment
Than a patiently accumulated savings account.)

Then one Sunday his reserve down-shifted to forlorn;
There were threats at home, a lockout, anger,
Fear, no breakfast, no lunch,
And a man living with them he considered his friend sent
 away.
I'd heard the troubled history, his return to his mother
Only sixteen months ago, her need for medication
And equal need, sometimes under-served, to avoid the
 booze.
He had come today not to visit but to escape.

He talked.
He talked with me.
He talked with a neighbor child who'd also come to watch
The latest construction stage on my winter wing
But then asked to be excused.

Something needed doing.
Hurried conversations with neighbors and relatives,
No dissent, only pleas for speed;
On Monday I invoked protection,
Alerted authorities to what I'd heard and seen,
More than any nine-year-old should carry;
By Wednesday he was gone.

He will never visit again,
His head cocked inside the biker's helmet
He was never without.

I did the *only* thing to do, really,
But once he'd gone doubt ripped like
Wolverine claws inside me.
Separating a mother from child is awful,
But so, then, is visiting fearful anger on a child.
Still, being spirited away to strangers has to terrify,
Leaving behind those tiniest of islands of stability and
       familiarity,
Even the broken, once-candy-filled glass Grumman F4F
We'd found together in the stream bed,
A treasure from fifty years ago,
Five-sixths my life but five *times* his.

> *When I wrote this poem ten years ago I was aware that both Balzac and Carver had connection to a similar experience. So that's how it got its title. Unfortunately, I didn't write the citation down. When I finally got to serious work on this volume I couldn't find the documentation. I realized I could have changed the poem's title and finessed the problem, but I chose to acknowledge the connection and absorb any possible embarrassment. Then, on Christmas day, 2009, in one of those incredibly fortuitous events that happen maybe thrice in a lifetime I opened a copy of the meticulously-documented biography by Carol Sklenicka,* Raymond Carver: A Writer's Life, *a gift from my youngest son. That led me to* All of Us, *Carver's collected poems (Knopf, 1998), and there I found 'Balzac' (p. 28). [Whew!] So I kept the title and fulfilled my academic obligations all at the same time. Of course, I then stayed with the collected poems for a couple of weeks and was struck by the frequency with which Carver wrote poems about the writing of poems. From a little hesitation about whether to include this poem, the deeper acquaintance reinforced my resolve.*

To Balzac and Ray Carver

Standing over the commode
Looking at my face perfectly reflected
In the mirrored flat of water
I was thinking how hard I must have struggled
With that poem
Not to notice for so long
How badly I had to piss.
So why aren't I now?
I'm reminded like a flash
How thinking's always been the
Tightest valve my bladder knows.

Relax. . .
Blank the mind. . .
Free the stream.

Like that(!)
My image is gone.

And just that fast the key
To the poem's lock
Popped into mind.

SIGHT

> *All winter in 2001 I walked daily on the streets of residential Cincinnati slowly rehabbing from a pair of back surgeries. I was puzzled all that time by the dozens and dozens of robins I kept seeing in large groups clustered in the strips between curbs and sidewalks and jammed into the young trees planted there. The experience resolved itself late one afternoon in a neighborhood Irish pub.*

Signals

Robins, it is said,
Are the harbingers of spring,
But several times
All winter long,
Sometimes in dense-twigged trees
With wizened deep-red fruit
Along the street
Or sometimes on the lawns and
Grassy strips between
The curb and walk,
I saw them swarm
In startling flocks of forty, fifty,
Or even seventy or more.

They say that robins
Are the heralds of spring,
But Melanie,
Leaning over the
Four-plays-for-a-dollar
CD jukebox at the "E"
In her spaghetti-strap

Black camisole
And her brunette tresses
Swishing lightly across
The unblemished skin of her back,
Works for me.

> *Writing poetry can be, variously, painful and sometimes just trying to walk a country road in the middle of mud-time. And sometimes it's just pure play!*

Variations on a Theme:
Axial Shift; the Spin to Spring
(A Haiku Sonata)

This morning's sun breaks
through the trees behind instead
of just beside me.

Late January's
sun, no longer at my side,
breaks past my shoulder.

Last month the sun struck
my cheek; today its rays fall
just behind my ear.

> *Senior year at Amherst I took my fiancé for a hike and spring picnic (a bottle of white wine in a thin wire wrap, a long baguette, cheese, and chocolate) up Mount Norwottuck, the highest point in Massachusetts' Holyoke Range. It was on that hike I saw the rusting sledge impaled by a heavy stand of laurel and set myself the challenge of writing a poem whose rhyme scheme evoked the timeless spirals of creation and decay.*

On a Twisted Sledge Norwottuck's Called to Rest

The earth calls back her own,
The straight now gray grain ages grown,
Iron bleeding into wood and ground.
(How dragged here, left near this peak so deep
Your crossbars split and weathered round?)
Now clasped by woodland's twisted laurel
The hands your bolts and runners forged
Thought not that death's decor be floral.
Your iron parts poured from the rock,
Wood struts conjured up from logs long felled,
Their wait through time inchoate for fate to knock
To claim you briefly, to shape, to use,
Then cast away, but not for nature to abuse.

> *Repeated exposure to something, something essentially unseen over and over again, is suddenly transformed by a seemingly stray thought. Of course, it isn't stray at all.*

Cemetery

In winter woods
deciduous leaves are gone
and all the brightness
opens deep lines of sight.
Mature snow
caps each of an entire cluster
of glacial erratics, their
mushroom umbrellas of white
held up by black faces of stone
no longer dusted
by a latest snowfall.
The stones stand
in memory of creatures of
an epoch now long gone.
There one marks a sabretooth,
here a camelops hesternus,
that huge one, perhaps,
a mastodon.
The master of them all,
that standing obelisk,
eight feet at its base,
upright another fourteen,
improbably erect
after ten millenia,
monuments the age.

Yet somewhere in the tiny sliver
of this century there
awaits a developer,
tractored cat deployed,
just the tool to knock it down,
force the stone aside,
or fill a void,
perhaps that last vernal pool.

> *Depending on bus transportation after years of commuting by car turned me into an observer as each day at roughly the same and always the same corner I waited for the next ride.*

Pigeons

The people waiting for the bus
Must have thought me, if not exactly crazy,
Slightly odd at least,
Me in adult-size child's frog hat with trailing legs,
Chin raised in rapt attention to parapets
Four stories up.
The pigeon flock, some fifty strong or more,
Had wheeled and turned,
Breathed in, breathed out,
Perhaps a dozen times above,
Sweeping cross the street, then high,
Beyond the facing roof
To re-emerge across the lot
Where grocery shoppers parked their cars,
Then pass above again and past the building line
To leave my line of sight.
How do they do it,
These fifty single birds
To seem to fly as one?
What magic makes them fly
As if guided by a single mind?
I slowly came to see
The flock wasn't stable after all,
As stragglers seemed to slip their links
And spin off like skaters

Lost to crack the whip.
Some cybernetics whiz
Or mathematics star
Must know the clue
To what it is that
Holds the members tip to tip.
Once more I watch the flock
Careen past me overhead
And just before they
Reach the rooftop's edge,
They brake in flight,
Tails wide and spreading down,
Wings scooping out the air in front,
The silhouettes of urban angels
Alighting silent just beyond my view.

> *The first attempt at this poem occurred more than a half dozen years before it was finally completed. Finishing it required the poet first to become comfortable with the possibilities of humor in poetry.*

Quiver

Hogan stands still,
His dark bulk parallel to the handrail
Feet firm in a couple of inches of new snow.
His head is slightly off line.
Nothing moves;
He seems to gives this quiet moment
Before dawn his total attention.
Nothing moves, I soon see, *except* the shiny black
Inverted apostrophes of his nose.

Etched by reflected light
Against the pure white of nightfall's snow,
His nostrils' black edges quiver,
Incline here, twitch there,
His snout steady, not risking
Any confusion of content or direction
As he picks the threads of the delicious messages
Borne to him on the morning's faintly stirring air.

I imagine those messages projecting
On cavernous screens in his mind:

Yesterday's repeated red squirrel taunts,
Their whip-cracking tail snaps,

The spruce-seed breath of their incessant chattering,
Well within teasing range but quite beyond capture;

Drifting signals of a fisher's meal of porcupine
Whose quills or excruciating slowness
On or off the ground had proved no deterrent at all;

A pregnant doe mincing her way
Across the road for browse or water;

Turkeys roosting in the trees,
Scat dropping on leaves frosted
By the lightly blown snow;

The huge white-banded black of the small herd
Of belted Galloways just up the road
Breaths and dung steaming in the rising morning air.

Hogan turns to look at me to question
If I really want him to go further.
"Get busy," I tell him, and he does,
And then comes hurrying back,
His eyes on mine the message clear:
"Enough of the movies; breakfast, please!"

> *Dmitri's, the Greek restaurant fronting on Connecticut Avenue in Washington, DC, is mirrored on both its side walls. This little ballet played out for me as I ate dinner one night and was then treated by the management to a complimentary Metaxa in recognition of my furious burst of writing to record its choreography.*

Dmitri's

They first came into view in mirrored glass
As through Dmitri's window they passed
From left to right, she, pretty, slight,
Round face, bubbling, her chest tight
To his broad back, hands flicking at his sides,
Though something said they'd rather play his thighs.

The two pass from view; I maintain my gaze,
And then an older woman takes their place,
Comfortable of build, seventy, I'd say,
She's made her Peter-Pan-collared way
From right to left, her gaze thrown to the rear
On the pair whose besotment was that clear.

She slowed her walk, turned more tightly
In her stare, but soon it softened; she lightly
Grinned, which then spilled wide,
As if to say she's satisfied
Her memories – and mine – grant clemency,
Two pardoned eavesdrops, not heard but seen,
As we both rode, in layered self-reflection,
Small thermals of remembered affection.

> *A bodacious storm, a watcher marveling at the awesome navigation and propulsion capacities of tiny birds, a comparison of their seeming unconcern, their undisturbed routines, with the worries the weather visits upon me.*

A Goldfinch and Edouard - September 2, 1996

Major wind gusts belch from the north
Bearing raindrops across the clearing
One side to the other without ever letting one set foot.
With grace equal to that power, you perch upon the thistle
    feeder
Bobbing gaily in the weather, following routine
Established in the weeks of summer.

Momentarily satisfied, you launch yourself,
Unerringly and unimpeded by the storm,
Your gold and black flitter-flitter swoop,
Flitter-flitter swoop, straight as an arrow
To the bending treetops from which you came.

You are in it and seem untouched;
I am sheltered from it
And still consumed by its implications.
Will the new roof and flashing remain tight?
Will the second anchor hold Scheveningen in Center Harbor?
Will tarps on the winter wing hold?
Shall I touch base with home in Ohio,
Let them know I'm holding up OK?

I make mental notes to load my chain saw in the truck
Before going off to supper with Becky,
Wondering whether I should even attempt the drive to Forest
    Farm
Given storm and bluster
Which seems to disturb you, Goldfinch, not at all.

> *More than fifty years ago in Freshman English we were given a writing assignment which obliged us to speculate on the meaning of a slowly evolving set of line drawings. Starting with just a few abstract lines, we were asked to look at the first and then each newly embellished configuration, describe what we saw, until each of us (at quite different points in the assignment, to be sure) finally recognized the oh-so-familiar structure which had remained unrecognized to us until that last sudden moment. I thought, as I have many times since then, of that exercise in language and meaning at the time of the experience recounted here.*

Confirmation

Four winters ago a sudden storm, a spruce-eater,
Blew up over Jericho Bay from the southeast
Laying down dozens of Brooklin's largest specimens
In widely scattered parallel tracks.

The 70-footer young Jason Milgram climbed in '89
Was one of the casualties, and in coming down it compounded
The hurt by halving the height of a twenty-foot pine
I'd planted, and since husbanded for nearly twenty years.

Not to be undone by the secondary harm,
And long a devotee of wolf pines, the next spring
I trimmed off the smashed trunk and tied the three branches
     just below into a bowl
To see if, in time, disaster could be turned into delight.

Observing the year's new growth this last July,
I felt satisfied my intrusion into nature had taken;
All three branches headed to the vertical.

Another year, I thought, I'll loose the ties I bound.

＊　＊　＊　＊　＊

And then this fall I saw the 18 inches of burned needles
Marking a pine weevil's deadly assault on one of the three
       leaders;
My first sense of dismay became instant exultation
At an insect's confirmation of July's judgment of success.

> *Mundane tasks, common encounters,*
> *compiled in patterns oft repeated can,*
> *nonetheless, be filled with surprise.*

Seasons Juxtaposed

I live in a clearing in the woods
A scant quarter mile as the raven flies
From the tidal flats of Herrick Bay
And so I've known for quite some time
That trees sweep water from the fog.
When in the fog roadside to the bay
I can fathom barely three car lengths ahead,
Across my clearing I can see
Each late season Canterbury bell,
The plumping pink of phlox,
The unfurling petals of the coming black-eyed Susans.

This morning, paint can, brush and drying towel
In hand and having seen the hints of sun
Break through the glowing fog,
I headed for the harbor to try and stem
The stubborn stain on my lobster cabin ceiling
By painting over suspect open pores
Upon the roof. I scrubbed the top,
Sluiced her clear, and toweled her off
And with the sun now breaking through
I left the roof to air dry and took
The dog to walk on Chatto Island.

At first I pleased us both by
Pitching sticks far out for Hogan to retrieve.
And when we tired of water play
I walked the back side of the island
Beach-combing as I like to do.
Back to the water, eyes toward the jagged line of tidal drift,
The now strong morning sun
On the island's towering spruces
Revealed they'd swept the now departed fog
Of a hundred thousand twinkling drops of water
Now glinting multicolor in the morning sun,
A stunning island stand of Christmas trees
Sparkling for just a moment
In an August morning's building heat.

> *Sometimes poems creep into your consciousness, sometimes they bang into you as in a pillow fight, and sometimes they flit past your eyes but manage to get a kind of harmonic going inside you, which in the subsequent moments, adds unanticipated depths to the original image.*

A Reading

The rain was intermittent,
The windshield wipers set the same,
And, befitting the weather,
The traveling pace restrained.
There was ample time, therefore,
To see the Bobcat loader
Angled toward me at the road's edge,
Its small headlamps lit, its bucket raised and,
In their bright wet-weather gear,
The two boys sat squeezed together
In the single bucket seat,
One lad slightly bigger,
Each inclined a bit toward the other
Making the most of the tight space they shared.
They seemed quiet,
Comfortable in the mist and with each other,
Both looking out to the busy roadway,
Protected in the Bobcat's wired cage, and –
Not altogether strangely,
It seemed to me the instant I'd driven past –
A loving family's matrix of

Boundaries, directions,
And sense of independence.

> *This all unfolded over the course of the time of the performance, and like stories we've all heard about how songwriters can sometimes pen a tune in a matter of minutes, except for later editing, this poem was written within an hour the next morning.*

Hands

Her face first touched me in the opera door,
Actually not her face at all -- that came later --
Just the side of her cheek, and abundant, framing, leonine
    hair.
I couldn't see her eyes or brow or lips;
I couldn't even catch a smile
If, in fact, she wore one, but something about
Her posture said care, intent, intensity.
By God, she really caught my eye!

I let the moment pass.

I showed my ticket; the taker waved me by.
I found my friends and took not my usual seat on an aisle
To serve my legs but one seat over
To be surrounded by my female friends. And Tim?
Well, he could just take the fourth seat in.
I turned left to him to talk
And caught my second glimpse of her,
Sliding in the very row the four of us had found.
I noticed -- but didn't, you know,
Reserve and sense of subtlety being what they are.
I'm still turned to speak with Tim,

And she leans out to speak with the person to her right.
We catch each other's glance, wide-eyed,
Full on, face to face, twelve feet apart.
I struggle, unobtrusively, I hope, to keep my cool,
A single moment, frozen in my time.

One of us turned away first -- I can't remember who.
I leaned back against the seat
Just head and eyes turned left.
I saw her forearm and her hand --
Gesturing,
Smoothing the program folder,
Resting on her thigh,
A thin hand, dark, I think, or, rather, tanned,
Tendons lightly raised fan-like on the back,
A gentle hand yet firm,
A hand that – odd thought – seemed somehow full of hope.

The performance closed.
I'd actually taken out a card to introduce myself,
An act so bold, so off my norm,
It quite filled me with surprise.

I hung back.
My party climbed the aisle.
I had her in my sight,
And then found her gone,
And then once more in view
Talking earnestly to a young man I knew.
Not daring to stare, I lost sight once more,
But he'd not left,

So I asked him who the woman was
On whom his attention centered.
He answered.
I grinned, felt foolish, turned red.
"Oh, that's my mom," he'd said.

> *This poem is one of several in the volume which portrays a person. It grew out of conversations I had over time with people who knew him and his history and wanted me to know of him, too, and finally I went to visit his granite garden, where I also met his artisan son who has now crafted some of the most dramatic and satisfying silver hair ornaments I wear.*

How Much More Do You Need to Know?

This former maker of rockets and stars;
A man of fancy;
A present-day gardener of rock,
Who cultivates his granite
And grows his obelisks and spires, his steps and pavers,
And schools still smaller stones to curves and spiral forms
That hold his flowers, squash, and more, tight to the living
      stone
And finds water for their lives in quarry filled;

Whose youngest child will etch and polish,
Or work with feathers, silver, shells, and such;

Who crafts great slabs for tables
To which only weighty matters will be taken
Next to a ring of fire and, just across the road,
A bandstand rising up with merry promise;

Who wants his granite garden to be a children's Mecca
For learning about land and stone,
And their hands and hearts;

And who, when his love passed,
Packed her ashes in a rocket and sent it aloft
Where his Liz "could paint his sky one more time."

> *My partner and I had taken a trip to Rangeley.
> We had seen her former summer cabin on West
> Richardson Pond. On the way back we stopped
> by a piece of property I had co-owned fifty years
> ago and hadn't seen in three decades.*

Time

Traveling west on 219,
Instead of angling off left
Parallel to the Nezinscot,
I drove us up the hill (still 219)
And then took the left
Below the church the sound of whose bell I helped liberate
One July 3rd night nearly half a century ago.

If the Grange coming up on the right
Had had a sign to that effect
It was now gone,
But the little hamlet into which we'd just driven
Seemed otherwise unchanged from fifty years ago;
The hard scrabble disrepair I remembered
Seemed somehow locked tight in time.

I knew this place.

At the edge of town we turned right,
Began the long climb up the road,
Though still gravel, significantly improved,
Maintained, even, up until the fork,
Where the A-frame had re-covered the cellar hole
Of the old farm house that had

Evaporated in flame that long ago winter night.

The half mile straight in to Damon Hill
Seemed suspended well into the last century.
The road gave every sign its bottom
Still disappeared each spring;
Here it was October,
Deep long puddles still marked its length,
And irregular ruts and ridges
Testifying to its often liquid state.

Imagine my surprise, therefore,
On encountering the now well-appointed
Spring house near the little crest above Damon Farm,
And the massive width of stone wall (new maybe not today
But certainly so within the span of years since last I was here)
Now marking the southwest corner of
The fresh-mown meadow running up the hill.
On the road's other side a well-tended lawn
And meadow below the house
Bespoke of the care bestowed this property
I'd given up in what I've often called another incarnation.

The old farm house that had been white
When another we of which I'd been apart
Had rescued it from going by
(And in whose other half's hands it still remains)
Was now a lovely ecru with
Faded apple green shutters.
The 1810 seven-room Cape (with attached el
And a rough hewn gambrel-roofed barn

Only months old when we bought it),
Had a double chimney resting on
A huge granite stonehenge cellar lintel.
To reach the bedrooms on the second floor
One climbed through the brick of the two pairs of separate
        flues on either side
Which arched over and then passed through the roof as one.

A brush wreath marked the dooryard entrance.
The clapboards appeared cleaner, straighter,
The chimney now well pointed,
And a screened-in porch had been added
To the southeast corner,
The very place where I'd had my last disabling asthma
Attack while scything down the raspberry profusion
Thriving where the then-recently-retired attached privy
Had been positioned.

> *Early on Captain Holland and I had raced against the*
>   *weather,*
> *Stripping off the decades old cedar shingle roof*
> *Held tight only by green moss whose matted surface*
> *Had been the house's sole protection against the rain.*
>
> *I had hauled the plate steel septic tank*
> *All the way from Cambridge,*
> *Dug out its resting place*
> *And then filled in the leach field trenches*
> *Entirely by hand.*
>
> *With Holland's help I'd blasted out a spring,*

Then built a dam and spillway to impound the pond
In which we'd waded seeking physical relief
From the shock of witnessing
Ruby murder Oswald
Before our very eyes that cold November day.

I recalled waiting .22 in hand at the southeast corner of the
        house
After red squirrels as they scampered
Down the shingled east wall.
(I never got them but Muffin, the money cat,
Dispatched them a little later all by herself.)
Muffin's roommate, Prudence, the grey Maine coon,
(Surprisingly in her case given her polished sedateness),
Had revealed similar skill the day
She'd been first released from apartment life
Presenting me within hours
Half each of a chipmunk, jay, and garter snake!

One snowy night I'd carried out
The still-burning Sears space heater
Its full tank, fuel expanding from warmth,
Beginning to spill out on the floor.

The afternoon we heard of Marilyn Monroe's death
We'd been skinny dipping in Pleasant Pond,
Our suits stripped off while swimming;
The narrow strip of beach
Lay right beside the road.

Later that fall I'd crouched for hours

Behind a log in the upper meadow
Overlooking deer paths in the alders just below
Waiting vainly for a shot,
An outdoor reward for having met my quota that day
Of ten pages of dissertation draft.

I remembered that old swamp Yank, Hoadley,
From whom we'd bought the place
Telling me as I unloaded from the car
Boxes of dissertation note cards
And volumes of primary source material
That if he'd known I "needed books you should have just
        asked.
I've got an attic full of them!"

I smelled again the scent of apples –
The still-bearing Mac's in front,
The almost impossibly hard Baldwins,
The heirloom sweet, oil-coated banana apples,
And the russets we'd cranked into gold-medal cider.

But it was the first stunning impression on
Seeing the farm after almost fifty years
That nearly trumped the memories.
Six white pine seedlings
I'd planted in barren lawn
Between the house and the road,
Had in those years transformed themselves to wolf pines
Twice taller than the power lines threading through them,
Not possible for me to reach around them,
Their diameters now a half again as thick

As those seedlings were tall
When first I placed them in the ground.

> *Poems are sometimes about parallels,*
> *events superimposed on one another,*
> *timely, however improbable. This is one.*

Fisher

The two streams sang thrush-like on either side.
I felt my cheek cradled under your arm nuzzling your neck.
As you stirred, too, I realized we'd both fallen asleep
Wrapped around each other on that sunny April afternoon
Under a light blue blanket deep in my woods.
An hour before we'd been hard at play,
Your hips drawn into me repeatedly at the end
Until my legs and thighs,
My lower back and then my shoulders
Became high voltage lines for vernal passion;
I relinquished myself to you.

Before the play,
In a moment of surprise, wonder and some uneasiness,
We'd watched a dark-hued fisher
With serpentine sureness and agility
Bound easily ahead of the pursuing but unseeing dog
Whose eyes and nose were occupied by scent instead of sight.
The fisher'd hopped the stream twelve feet from us,
Leapt directly onto a spruce and shot up thirty feet,
Sliding easily from one to another
Of the closely neighboring trees and
Ending up looking down,
Draped deliberately on a branch
In a cross-pawed posture of repose.

> *I had returned home to our summer place in Maine and was busily opening the house and getting ready for my family, and then grief over my brother's death came to call once more.*

Grief's Bad Penny

My third day in Brooklin,
Month four since Marty's death,
I felt (I thought) that time at last
Was lending healing calm;
I had this sense of slowly growing ease
Foreseeing saying, in days just ahead,
The poem I'd written to celebrate,
With family and friends, my brother's life.

I raised the porch screens,
Hung the Carolina hammock,
Visited last year's building project,
And cleared away the winter boughs,
And in these acts I suddenly came to see him
As he was last August,
Standing tall and only faintly ill,
Throwing balls to tireless Vixen
(I'd found two when clearing boughs!),
And lying back, arm over head,
Glasses on his nose and novel in hand,
And helping carry boards to Becky's cabin.

In my vision he was whole again,

Not the husk, by fall, he had become,
And grief returned in full,
Not yet begun to ease at all.

> *This probably means more to me than it will to most who might read it, but though it happened nearly ten years ago the 500 words it takes to tell evoke the memories, despite all the intervening personal and political nightmares, as if they were yesterday. It's my volume, though; I can include it if I want, and so I do.*

Thanksgiving Gift, 2000

On Wednesday early evening,
In the single hour to pass
Before the three of us would
Sit to sup on tiny new potatoes,
Baked salmon, and salad many-hued,
I set out on a two-mile walk,
My twice-a-day recovery stroll
That followed on the reaming out
Of lumbar disks five weeks ago.

It's dark; the twenty blocks I start to walk
Are full of tiny houses
So much the style north of Detroit.
I take a turn and see a light
Spill from a large bay window
Consuming nearly half the front façade,
And as I start to draw abreast I realize
I see a large neat kitchen, full of light.
The woman of the house, or so I took her,
Sat at the table facing out,
Absorbed by reading matter in her hands.

The room so bright and open
To the street reminded me of
Scenes like this
I'd seen on trips to Holland,
My father's land,
He gone, now, fifteen years.

The warmth of what I'd seen
Stayed with me through the frigid air
That bathed the walking therapy
On which I had embarked.
At supper I told the twins
The happy thoughts that moving glimpse
Had given me.

Thanksgiving morn
I placed the heaping apple pie to bake
And set the clock for eighty minutes hence.
I used the time to retrace steps.
Now streets are brilliant, sunny, bright,
And yards which had been empty, dark the night before,
Now harbored iron horses tethered
Single, double, triple file
Beside the modest homes.
I walked and thought it might be nice
To thank the home for happy thoughts
It brought to mind, and
So I searched out the cheery kitchen bay,
And turned the corner on their drive,
My smile a greeting to the daughter and her dog
Who sat behind the glass.
I rang the bell,

And when the woman I had seen last night
Opened up the door, I told her what I'd seen
And gave my thanks for what she'd given me.
She listened with a widening smile
And finally said to me "How sweet,"
And wishing her a happy day
I let the outer door spring closed
But not before I left behind
A smile of my own.

I reached my outbound goal,
And turned the mid-walk loop
To put the sun and wind behind me.
No sooner had I done than ten feet up ahead
A copper glint told me a penny'd dropped.
Three steps I was upon it, and
Looking down I realized at once
The five feet from my eyes to ground
Seemed somehow further now my disks had been re-done.
Were the coin a ballot –
The language of electoral impasse
Fair nearly jumped to mind –
I'd sure not let it lie.
And slowly bending from the knees,
I deftly doffed my glove, and
Pressing down my thumb and slipping
Index nail beneath the rim,
I pocketed the shiny coin.
I wondered how many more such 'votes'
My walk might yet disclose;
Was it an omen there weren't more?

Hoping not I took my key and entered in
The richly scented apple air of the
First kitchen I'd left that day.

The poem below was among the very first I wrote; it has the distinction of being the only one I can recite from memory. But each time I do so it does something for me that it can't possibly do for anyone else (except, now, for this introduction). It reminds me of a room I lived in for a year, 1955-6, as a sophomore at Amherst. I had a small painted turtle (now long unavailable in pet stores for health reasons). The turtle occupied a modest size bowl with a basking stone, living greens, and frequently changed water. It sat on a Chinese red, flat black, and gold-trimmed table I had built myself. It was a time which marked the single greatest transformation of my life as I really took hold of my academic career and, much to my everlasting surprise, began to become a quite successful varsity swimmer following a childhood characterized by asthma, allergies, and physical weakness. The poem is included because it was near the beginning, because it was so tiny — like a seed, and because it had essentials of form, structure, meter, and rhyme in contrast with so much of what was to follow.

Symmetry

My turtle's means of motion
Aren't fit for the ocean
But rather the role
Of life in a bowl.

ACTION

> *Judi Beach, as I noted in my dedication to this volume, was a poet of substance. She could take the simplest, most every day aspects of life and weld them into evocations of universality even as they were deeply grounded in the specificity of an individual lived life. We were members of the evening Deer Isle writing group. I came to her attention before I had written very much myself because she valued my observations on her poetry. Over the years she assumed an ever more central place in that small group of people every lucky poet finds whose counsel proves invariably helpful. The loss I feel is immense.*

Her Voice is Not Stilled

Some things happen way too fast.
Between hearing the worst
And now standing with others in the garden
As her son, Jason, spreads her ashes,
It has been fewer days than the number of blades
Of any single one of the young lupine leaves wavering before
    me.
I feel some awkwardness, though;
Deep sadness struggles with satisfaction
That I'd taken the chance during that eyeblink of time
Before her voice was stilled to tell her how
I'd thought of her as my mentor for ten years,
How I'd thrived under her precise, yet gentle attention,
Drawing out of me what was already there
Even if neither of us could recognize it until it finally
    emerged.

"You helped me find my voice, " I told her.
She'd acknowledged my thanks
With an insistent expectation,
Steely despite her faint hold on life,
That I carry my work forward to fruition.

A light rain falls.
The vigorous clump of lupine before me bobs randomly
As isolated drops hit now one, then another,
Of individual blades of the palmate leaves,
Turning it into a multi-tongued jew's harp
Playing out a melody
Just under the voices of other friends
Speaking Quaker style of what she'd meant to them.
The lupine tongues are playing a tune she's written
I can't quite grasp, and instantly I know it
I hear her saying to me
"That's your task, Hendrik, that's your job.
Transcribe the tune,
Transform it into words uniquely yours,
And sing it for your friends."

Her voice is *not* stilled;
It guides my wordway as I go.

> *In my early fifties I discovered both a passion and penchant for building. This is the only poem I have written so far about my own building experiences. The poem's structure actually began with the experience recorded in the last stanza, and the poem construction process worked methodically backward from that single image . . . not unlike the planning process for any building or structure once its final shape is configured. The finished product, quite central to my weekly life, is depicted on the back cover, and the outline of its door inspired the Gandalf Press logo.*

Glow

Between mid-April and the end of August
I built a poem in three dimensions,
A sauna on a now green hill, but once clay gray.
Behind its live-edged siding
Sawn from trees taken
For the pond the sauna oversees,
Ohio cedar reigns supreme –
Shiplap siding where shoulders lean,
One inch sanded runners to sit upon,
And everywhere that one can see
The symmetry of clapboards' textures
Please the eye.

And then the door,
The door,
An oh-so-simple notion born of a tandem trunk
That stood upright as if to say "please use,"
Like a line I could not lose.
It was months before its place
Would finally fit,
For nested puzzles,

Almost without number,
Fell from my naive conceit
The inverted "n" the trunks subscribed
Could frame, perhaps, the entry to my poem.

The curves that double spruce embraced
Ran short and long,
Compound and straight,
In several planes.
Completion of the framing plan
That grew inexorably,
Step by step –
With no more notion
Of the one beyond
Than how a poem grows –
Took many working days.

The key lay in adding other wood
As magic as a poem's just-right word –
Red oak to sculpt jambs
Anchored deep into the spruce
To hold the clamps to cold mold
Narrow strips and resin
To shape the door's internal frame . . .
Which formed, and set, and joined across,
Could ground a cedar skin,
A starburst, white and red,
Exploding on the door
As if to say, the heat inside
Came from our sun
And also all who enter here.

I sit at the corner of the house
Writing this poem about my poem.
September's sun has lowered its sights

Just enough to bathe the sauna's door in
Light so purely gold it makes me catch my breath.

> *There is one building of the fifteen on my place I didn't build. I designed it for my goddaughter and her partner; the challenge for me was to draw something that met their specifications but which they, almost totally naive to construction, could understand as well as acquire skills on-the-run sufficient to complete the task. I taught, explained, demonstrated, and then watched as Becky and Cynthia built and enclosed "Small Moose Lodge" in the three and a half weeks available to them.*

Love Abuilding

Becky's feet stand placed
between post "A" and beam "G"
her back arched over intently,
butt close to her heels.
Cynthia's feet stand just outside the frame,
her back straight, head down;
the orange stripes on shirttails
borrowed from the godfather-in-law
(to keep off bugs, you see,
just as they had him for years
and no doubt would for more)
whip in the early evening wind.
Now crouched together above the frame,
they seek to measure, fit, cut, raise,
and enclose in just one month.
One hand clasps tape,
a second the square,
a third holds post on beam,
a fourth scribes on the line
defined by the post's edge,
"four inches and a quarter

minus a sixteenth."
Their hands and forearms
intertwine at angles acute,
making teepees of care and affection
to craft a cabin that soon will rise
in a wooded sepulchre
first seen and then chosen by her
only several months before.

> *Ralph is still fixing things, most currently helping the public retrofit their homes to improve energy efficiency. The organization memorialized here, however, despite our best efforts, could not overcome its inherent flaws.*

Ralph

There we were in the frigid black of a winter night,
Getting ready to drive off for supper
Before the evening meeting of the Board;
The prospect of that gathering was
At least as unsettling to our stomachs
As their emptiness.
As I sat next to him in the car dark I asked
About the strange black cable coming out of the
Cigarette lighter and he allowed as how
It was connected to a voltameter just below (see?),
And then he launched into a long dissertation
I barely understood about how his alternator
Was acting badly and if he didn't monitor
Its current outflow carefully he could start the car and
Get it to where he was going,
But because of the alternator's failure to recharge the battery,
The car would not start again . . .
But, he continued, he'd also discovered through many trials
    and error
That if he smacked the alternator upside its head
With a hammer he could coax it to perform.

No one asked him how he'd discovered that.
But we didn't really have time because he'd started the car,
Asked if I could read the gauge (then registering 10 or 11
    somethings)
And would I tell him after he'd performed his little operation

84

Whether it was now reading a proper 13 or 14.
I bobbed my head up and down to figure out which layer
Of my trifocal lens would give me the best reception in the
	gloom,
Said yes I could, and out he went into the dark, hammer in
	hand.
He raised the hood, leaned in, and began thunking.
I began calling out the rising indicator –
Twelve two, twelve eight, thirteen four –
And by the fourth hit it was fourteen two.
Ralph lowered the hood, climbed in the car, and we set off to
	eat.

We held our strategy session, ate our meal, headed back for
	the car.
And repeated the drill; this time I knew what was expected of
	me.
Ralph climbed back out hammer once again in hand,
Raised the hood, and I began announcing values
While Ralph thunked away until they rose again.
There was great good humor, palpable relief in the vehicle,
As we laughed over the improbabilities of hammering out
	power
From a reluctant piece of machinery.

Walking up the broad stone steps to the meeting
I wondered where the alternator in our organization was,
Who would be minding the voltameter, and if,
In our collective hands, the hammer we had fashioned over
	supper
Would be wielded with Ralph's similar resolve, reserve, and
	result.

> *Blue Hill peninsula poets were urged to express our views on the inexorable march toward war with Iraq promulgated by Bush, Cheney, Rumsfeld, and the neo-cons. From the perspective of all that happened in the seven years that followed this now strikes me as tame.*

Where Will It End?

Two score years ago, nearly,
For months on end it seemed,
I stood on sidewalks in the nation's capital
Carrying signs knowing I was being filmed
By agents of the FBI in their slowly circling
Smoked-glass paneled trucks
Keeping tabs on Feds like us who came out at lunch
To speak our piece for peace.
The weekend images of hedgerows
Of Boone's Farm Apple bottle green,
Campfires on the mall,
The flowing gowns of monster puppets
Gliding down Pennsylvania Avenue,
The hovering haze of a thousand lit torpedoes
Under Tecumseh's knowing gaze,
The scary roar of Huey's rearing up across the mall
At treetop level as Pentagon jockeys tried
To put the fear of God into tens of thousands
Assembled to make our leaders listen --
I remember it well.

I thought I was done with all that because
America was done with all that,
But here I am, now well into my sixties
Writing the Chancellor of Germany and the President of
    France

Imploring them to do what they can
To stop my country from starting, alone, a war
With implications beyond imagination
Because my president won't listen,
Can't understand.
I send my half-cup bags of rice
To feed our enemies rather than fire upon them,
Post signs,
Spend treasure to air a Sunday ad in Washington
To reach the football fan at Camp David,
Embrace the rapid protest of the digital revolution,
Appending my name, rank, and serial number
To every e-mail I send out
So Poindexter and Company in the Pentagon
Don't waste time and taxes figuring out just who I am,
So they can find me if they really want.

Otherwise life is good;
My country and I have had
A good reciprocal run of things.
But truly I am embarrassed, now, to be a bully,
To hear my world-wandering friends
Talk of traveling as the Greeks or Russians they once were
Or as Canadians they might pretend to be,
To say nothing of my chagrin at listening over potluck after
    sauna
To counsel we should be reading Gibbon on Rome
To understand our neo-Texan emperor at home.

> *I occasionally wonder whether there's any experience available to humankind whose meaning can't be focused by an attempt to apply poetic principles in its expression. After telling this once, then writing it down in two different forms as feedback to my medical professionals and then repeatedly relating to curious friends and acquaintances the several levels of surprises the story encompassed, I made this attempt and I sent it off to JAMA. The poetry editor dismissed it out of hand saying it wasn't really poetry. Perhaps. Her assessment, however, counted for naught in deciding whether I should include it here.*

Faithful to the Core

The IV drips morphine, dextrose,
A pair of powerful antibiotics.
The excruciating pain
Has lost its edge but
Bloat, dizziness, and
A sense of absent elements of
A capacity for sequential thought
Have taken up residence in its place.

Four days I've been here,
Each morning a different struggle
With changing medical staff
Over maintenance meds I'd taken
Special care to bring along with me.
Intake confirmed I'd done right,
But day followed day
With changing sets of puzzles:
What of my meds I'd be allowed to take;
What changes to accept;
What unknown substitutes to
My long validated regimen to mull;

And risking a 'troublesome' label
For failing to comply.
Pain spiked my glucose, too;
Insulin was prescribed, administered once,
Yet the juices I was finally given
(After 36 hours of nothing,
not even water, to slow my system down)
Were full of sugar, and the food tray
(When I finally got one)
Had huge double desserts,
And not once a sugar substitute thereon.
My malady (a name too cumbersome for verse;
I came to think of it as appendicitis on the other side)
Called for reduced fibre for a while.
So who OK'd the Raisin Bran,
And while, for lunch, the sparely steamed,
Lemon-dripped broccoli was delicious,
Not until more research at home did I learn
Any brassica was problematic for a time.

Before I left I told this triple tale of conflict,
Inconsistency, failure to cohere.
The doctor said write it down; I did.

I learned one thing last week;
No matter how far down a bug might take me,
The analyst inside does not desert.
And was reminded of two others:
Unconscious stress can harm; and
Never miss an offered chance to serve.

> *Eliot Coleman is a hero to many; even I think so and I don't even have to discount his graduation from Williams to do so. My privilege has been to observe him for years as part of a fluctuating group of organic farmers, artisans, and craftsmen (and women!) who have convened themselves for an unbroken series of saunas and potluck suppers for over 30 years.*

In Praise of Small Packages

So there he was, this impish little boy masquerading as a man,
Standing before the fireplace with its large stone heart.
He was making a little like a pontiff, you know,
And the rest of the assembly, warmed by a sauna
Unusually hot, fresh from a meal up to every expectation,
And maybe three, four (many?) bottles of wine,
Began a shower of take-down-a-peg zingers.
From every corner in the room,
The sustained volley outlasting any Connors and McEnroe
Gave us all those years they were at the top,
Its finesse displayed in the ways the lines and nets
Shifted swiftly to conform to the source of the latest barb.
And still the bantam hero fielded every shot,
A tour de force, so light, so sharp,
Informed by years of shared experience,
Full of love, humor, and affection,
Leaving no one in the room not feeling royally entertained.

I've only occasionally thought outside the box [!] when it comes to placing poems on the page, but this is clearly one of them. I had just finished being the focus for a particularly virulent irrationality and hatefulness in town, a function of my believing, as a Selectman, in orderly procedures, feedback, writing things down, accountability, and the rule of law all of which, in our case, meant necessary change. When a small group of people experienced discomfort (embarrassment might be a more precise term) at the resulting illumination, their almost instinctual discomfort for change of familiar process no matter how flawed spurred them to rebel. Following the ensuing active rejection of my two elected "colleagues" on town council, it became clear to me, much as I loved the work (which proved, by subsequent events, to have a substantial and lasting effect beyond the two years of my labor), municipal government would shut down if I didn't step aside. I did. I'm proud of two things, though: I never lost my cool nor my sense of humor, and I have continued to serve the town both as an observer and a substantive contributor.

Mycelium: My Town

I would harvest for the
people the outcomes of close attendance to the surround
and careful meditation thereon, but it's like knowing there are mycelia
down there somewhere beneath the composting mulch of public
need and desire and
trying to guess when
mushrooms'
caps will
first break
through, in what
shape, what color,
and where.

> *Driving to Ellsworth one morning I felt assaulted by the sudden appearance of newly minted road name signs bright red, a color I'd never before seen used for that purpose. And then the apparent egotism revealed rankled me even more. The county newspaper of record published this immediately.*

Waylaid

'Ginny May's Way.'
'Nancy's Way.'
'Theresa's Way.'

Red signs
suddenly appear,
ways out of place.

Why red?
What logic
decreed street
signs created
to address
emergencies,
should cause the
names of roads
to sport the
color tone of danger,
thus making
apprehension
the guiding image
for our sense of place?
(Of course, the brightness
of the green
that's also used

is not much better;
the posting of the
names of roads
in Holbrook
Sanctuary
have turned it into
just another
subdivision.)

And how about
the pomposity
of "Way"?
One visions
Roman legions
around the bend
just out of sight
and if you'd stop
to listen
you might just hear
the ordered march
of ten thousand
muffled sandals
preparing to lay siege
to High Street.

How odd that this
should happen here.
We've had the smarts
to ban the
billboard ads
that other states
mistakenly
feel feed their
economic health,
but now authority
has conspired

with ego
to render place
a pain in more
than just one way,
a blight brought on
this rural scene,
unforeseen
accidents at
intersections of
roads called
'Technology,'
'Bureaucracy,'
'Vanity,'
and 'Fear.'

Wrong way.

No way.

Go 'way.

> *This title is a play on words of a mantra I first found myself intoning during a difficult policy assignment at the time of my first administrative responsibilities in the 1960's. "Leaving Tracks" invoked the idea of taking good minutes, writing thorough debriefing memos after meetings, and undertaking policy studies to establish and document current situations as a basis for thinking systematically about what to do next. Sometimes when one's head finds itself functioning at times when it "really hadn't oughter be," amusement flows.*

Loving Tracks

Squeezed together
In the narrow berth
Of the sleeper hurtling west,
We giggled at the thought
We should have
Logged our journey,
A little pin
Impaling each point on the track
Where our loins joined
Or lips had clasped one another
In earthly delight.
We laughed at our failure
To acquire the system map
And stopping at Staples
To lay in a proper pushpin supply.

> *I suppose this could have been subtitled 'once a planner, always a planner,' but it's another example of just how deeply rooted are the fundamental structures of one's persona.*

Still Type A
With a tip of the hat to E.B. White

Two gorgeous days are promised us today and tomorrow.
I might fork over the French bed with new compost
Getting ready to plant next year's garlic.
I could dig the shallots and lay them out to dry,
Or do a last weeding of the raised vegetable beds.
I could take the come-along and pry bar and pull out the
      three stumps
And the buried rock in the space under my new woodshed,
But I'll need to haul fill for the stump and rock holes
And then move the ten pallets into place.
I could nail down its eight roof panels.
I could collect the tools from building and replace them in
      the barn.
The repaired rollers could be re-attached to the trailer.
There's laundry to do and two days of dishes to wash.
I could print out multiple copies of a couple of recent drafts
      and go to writers',
And then there's that appointment with the eye doctor,
And the Solid Waste Committee meeting to monitor
      tomorrow night.
I could take a healthy bite out of the spread sheet research on
      the transfer station tasks.

I could start little tasks I've been saving – sanding new
      walking sticks,

Making the sign for Alison proclaiming Yogi's presence in the
    shop . . . or not.
I could remind myself not to worry about the surgery the day
    after tomorrow.
I could weed the loam pile and split for the sauna the thirty
    pieces of trunk wood
I cut from the dead trees surrounding my winter house
My eldest helped me take down last summer.
I could purchase and place the rolls of 30# felt for the
    woodshed roof
And do one last string trim of the perennial beds on the
    edges of the lawn

Yes, I might do those things . . .

[*Surgery Wednesday. . .?*
No lifting for at least two weeks,
Maybe four. . .?]

Oh dear . . . I did them all!

These are the remarks I delivered February 13, 1995, as discussant of three papers presented by close friends and deep collaborators on a multi-institution teacher education initiative known as the Holmes Group. Holmes attempted to further advance the reform of teacher education by engaging graduate institutions presumably closely immersed in research about education and instructional practice in full partnership with public schools. On several different levels it was controversial and risky, and "huddling together for warmth" was one of the key tactics which kept us going. I had retired as the University of Cincinnati Dean of Education nine years before, but one of my conditions on not taking yet another reappointment after nearly fifteen years was the university's willingness to search for my replacement using as one criterion the successful candidate's commitment to participating in Holmes. I returned to the faculty and became a deeply committed "mule" to carry the work forward in the university and the Cincinnati Public Schools. At the time that I was asked to be the discussant for three papers by Chuck Case and Dick Wisniewski, colleague deans at the Universities of Connecticut and Tennessee, and Bob Yinger, the Director of the Cincinnati Initiative for Teacher Education (the name of our Holmes effort) and later Dean at Baylor, I was myself coordinator of Cincinnati's new secondary teacher education program, then in the final stages of implementation. Its central features were a five year commitment, dual degrees in Arts and Sciences and Education, and a paid internship in Professional Practice Teams where fifth year interns were guided by master teachers, three career teachers, and a university faculty member. The program was fabulously successful, if very hard work, and a constant struggle against considerable odds imposed by the conflicting norms resident in the collaborating institutions and their several actors. The proof was in the pudding, though; the employment placement rate for the first year graduates was 100% as compared with barely 60 percent for the last year of the old program; school principals and superintendents knew the program and wanted its products.

When I read the three papers to prepare for my remarks, I found there was nothing I could add. The program outlines were clear, the struggles documented, the reflections merited by the work. I couldn't figure out what I might add until, casting about for anything, I picked up the Gideon (!) Bible in my hotel room, happened to open it to Job, and therein germinated the seed for the benediction which follows. To speak poetically in an academic setting would be risky under normal circumstances, but I was among friends, a year from retirement, and it was not the first time I'd paid heed to other drummers. Unfortunately, for the reasons mentioned above, only tiny vestiges remain of what we accomplished at Cincinnati. I'm glad I didn't have to witness its slow death.

There Are Others

"Then will I also confess unto thee that thine own right hand can save thee." (Job 40:14)

There are others.
And they shall be called kin.
There are others,
And by their parallel covenants shall they be known.
There are others,
And amid slowly rising expectations,
The revolution shall be born.

There are others.
And their separate stories shall be seen as one.
There are others,
And by their patience shall they be known to you.
Their endurance clothes them,
And they shall be found frequenting many places
Where once they dwelled in splendid isolation.

There are others,
And knowledge of their presence
Girds even those in the farthest reaches of the land.
There are others,
And in the quiet ferocity of their knowledge
That the more you know, the more you need to know,
Burns fuel for their journey.

There are others,
And the quiet succor they lend one to another --
Tribe to tribe,
Camel to sheep,
Even oxen to ass --
Assures mountains will bring them forth food and
Fields will be found where all the beasts can play.

There are others
And where the people rise up out of whence they came
And wrap themselves in clothing
Woven from one another's flax on one another's looms,
And feed themselves from the bread and vessels of the tribes
With whom they would build their covenants,
There shall we find them.

There are others,
And they have learned that time is an ally
Whose passing must be sheltered
By a commonly raised and commodious tent of promise,
A passing exalted by continuous action,
No matter its modest cast,
Each deed building unto the one that follows.

There are others,
And if in the beginning there was the word,
In the middle and in the end
There must be the deeds,
And in the knowledge that to decide is not necessarily to do,
But to do is to decide,
Great works have been begun.

There are others,
And they have come to know
That the carefully crafted maps of the land of Uz we knew
Will not guide us in the land of promise we devoutly seek.
Old eyes must be set to seeing once again,
And new parchment prepared,
And new marks entered thereon
As we learn the valleys, streams, and hills ahead.

There are others,
And those who you heard this morning are among their number.

There are others,
And in that certain knowledge there is hope.
There are others,
And in their presence I know awe, and comfort, and community.

And the Lord said to these others, these descendants of Job,
Even as he said to the patriarch,
"Then will I also confess unto thee that thine own right hand can save thee."

PATIENCE

> *Voices can be found almost anywhere, in this case emanating from a mammoth jade tree sitting in the southwest corner of a homesteaders' abode on Cape Rosier.*

Telltales

Wide as my hand can span, the light brown trunk
Lifts limbs that hold eight spreading feet
Of jade leaves five feet deep.
Its start was here; it thrived and has for long.
Throughout its life in Harborside.
In all the years no frost has ever filled this space.
No Daniel Pat could claim benign neglect for you,
No chance missed to house your roots in ever larger pots.
No other site but prime south light,
The corner window where you sit, large,
Perhaps the outward views sacrificed
To admit inward flows of light to fuel your patient growth,
The stage in which you sit --
Soft tones of wood, of candle glow,
Of spirited talk from steam-cleaned souls,
Good food and wine,
The warming irony of the chimney's centered heart of stone –
Testifies to care bestowed,
To patience and design in lives that place home
In stead of nothing else.

> *In Maine spring arrives weeks and weeks after everywhere else in the lower 48. The next two poems try to capture some of the cruelty of thinking of March as the month when spring debuts in the face of the reality that our daffodils often don't appear until later April and trees are not fully leafed out sometimes until the beginning of June.*

An Existential Moment Slow to Come

Spring this year was slug-like,
An interminable overture
To the longed-for music of summer.
The first nubs of April green,
Tipped yellow from the frequent early freezes,
Didn't push their way through leaves and ground
Until mid-month and even then
The upward thrusts proved snail-like, too --
An eighth inch a day,
Sometimes a quarter,
And sometimes none.
One day, though, they grew an inch,
The next another, and then a third,
But the skinny slips of buds
Proved faint promises
Wraith-like as they were.
By April 20 they'd reached their proper height
But still thin, Twiggy-like,
And proudly straight without a hint of
Dipping down to proper tilt for daffodils.

A day later their first small sign of letting down,
The next day off vertical to one o'clock,
And then two, and finally three.
The buds began to fatten,
The temperature hit seventy
And still they held back,
But on the 28th the first trumpet
Blared out its golden sound;
And the very next day the entire brass
Ensemble played out its joy,
As Baba Ram Dass would say,
At being here now.

> *The length of a poem bears no relationship whatsoever to the ease with which it is generated. I chose the form for reasons obvious to its content, but then accomplishing the objective became something of a nightmare.*

Haiku for a Truncated Spring

(Brooklin, Maine, June 1-2, 2005)

Yesterday no shade;
Today no sun's ray touches
The tree-covered drive.

> *How I approached participation in my brother's memorial service.*

Puzzles

I went that last December week to Boston
To share in what I hoped would be
My brother's convalescence
Only to discover I would instead,
With precious others,
Be helping Marty through his death.

And his passage was with grace,
With warmth and confidence,
And awe-ful style,
And he accepted the end,
Finally, almost as a gift.

      1.

But it was his to have just once;
We live it over and again.

      2.

He used to tell his family and friends
The Christmas gifts I gave him were "puzzles."
He would look at them this way and that,
Marvel with an eyebrow raised,
And then ensconce them on his mantel,
All the while returning favors not dissimilar.

3.

We both sailed often
(In our respective boats and waters, though),
Yet I just once with him,
And he barely more than that with me.

4.

We were not close . . .
He lived a thousand miles away.
But we were so firmly fixed
In each other's firmament,
That neither of us did anything, really,
Without the referent of the other.
(We have our parents in part to thank for that.
Identity for us both came to depend upon
Successfully reading the subliminal
And never letting our vision ignore the peripheral.)

5.

He called my Hendrik the obedient son,
But it was Marty who carried our parents
Safely through their waning years.

6.

We knew each other from our respective
Beginnings sixteen months apart;
He now leaves me an orphan and the patriarch,

A juxtaposition he would have laughed over
Had I thought it to share with him as we talked
The days before he died.
How brilliant those last moments,
Shared,
Back home at the last for several days,
Buoyed by exquisite space,
Sky lit, sun bathed,
Moon and music washed,
Always lucid, warm, and caring,
Talk metered out to us
To save the slowly ebbing strength
To say what needed saying,
To hear what others' need say to him,
Absorbing, grasping,
Becoming comfortable
With the occasional surprise,
To him as well as others.

7.

He shared with me a thought
I thought I'd keep for us alone
Until I found he'd written it to us all
The day before to be delivered
Four weeks almost to the day he left us.
"I haven't been a very good brother,"
He said to me, I tearfully astounded,
Having come resolved, whatever outcome
Might emerge, to tell him of the
Hero status he held for me arising from
His selfless embrace of Angie and Celeste

("Oh, no," he said, so fast,
Characteristically uncomfortable
With my assignment,
"It was a privilege I've
Been lucky to enjoy.")
And how I had for decades
Described to others
But never shared with him
How Marty was the family missionary,
Serving sinners in the courts
With no less zeal or dedication
Than any cleric might have mustered.
(His response to that?
A quick embarrassed smile.)
He did not leave believing what he wrote to all
And what he'd said to me alone;
What worried him I think I laid to rest
By what we talked about at last
And now can safely lay to rest with him.

        8.

For three days after he was gone
His son and I retrieved and boxed
The records of career to
Pass batons to others who'd agreed
To carry on the cases unresolved.
No ease in that task, I'll say.
Addressing Marty's varied strategies
To keep, stack, enclose,
And only sometimes file,

Sparked inner irritations — and then guilt —
Until I came to see that serving
What seemed, at first, a disarray
Was but a metaphor for
Starting to address the mess in me.

        9.

A thousand miles apart for nearly thirty years
(Half life it was, to take a term from physics)
Yet at the end, we seven —
Brother, son, our wives,
And daughters three —
Linked by touch to him —
And equally with each other —
Vouchsafed him on the final voyage
To moor him in our hearts forever.
At end he'd gathered all life's threads,
Tying off his tapestry,
And then he fixed those threads
From his life's loom to ours,
Binding us together, one to the others,
Others to each one,
To savor new futures
He assured us we would have
Through his benediction.

> *One of those golden moments that if it weren't written down would more than likely be lost altogether. Is this the other half of a binary star with 'Dandelion Seed Puffs' (p. 162)? But of course!*

Of Maple Syrup and Dandelions Gone to Seed

Your skin glows amber,
The candles surrounding us
Taking all your gentle curves
To their illogical extreme
With promises to let me taste
The history of hidden fire
In the syrup that is you.

The miracle?
The achenes that are you
Merge perfectly
With the achenes that are me
Yet when we,
Now and again,
Momentarily drift apart
Our capitulums stay whole,
Unbent,
Unruffled,
Undisturbed.

> *How could a poet not write about moments like these?*

Respiration

Breathe in the scents of you,
The flowers of your skin
That bloom above my passing pursing lips,
Aromas casting tints that fill the
Palette just behind my eyes
And seep into my cup of quiet time with you.
My fingers trail surfaces familiar in their form
But new in you now here with me --
The hollow just inside your knee,
The one your arm and breast define,
The smell of sun upon your wrist,
Sweet taste of morning sweat,
The herbal hint above your ear,
The musk that draws me now – and then again –
And then yields me leaning back to drink you in,
My eyes now taking up
What lips and breath have just released.

> *This poem began with the Lenten image of hot cross buns and recognition that it was still a good four weeks away.*

Mid January, the Coast of Maine

For two days the weather maps have been
Covered with zeroes and negative numbers.
I walk on the now densely packed frigid snow
To the newspaper box at the end of the driveway
On laced up boots whose bites each step
Bark sharply into the adjacent woods.
The banks of snow on either side
Are stained with bursts of neon yellow
From Hogan's frequent visits
To assure the rest of Brooklin's dogs,
Whether or not they ever show, this is his wintery turf,
But its startling contrast to the blinding white
Makes me think of sunflowers and
Black-eyed Susans seven months to come.
It's cold all right;
A moment is all it takes for my beard to ice over
Into a chilled Kurly Kate glued tape-like round my mouth.
The days are finally longer at both ends, not just one;
Our collective thirst for light built from its inexorable
        withdrawal
Ranks that welcome change first in conversation queues.
My eyes sting, though, from sleep lost last night
Rising every two hours to stoke the stove;
Damping-down no longer serves.

Despite the roundness of my house,
And the tightness of its design,
The cold is so quiet and deep
It steeps the heat out in moments
Like boiling water teases tea
From the Constant Comment bag.
The thick flaking sugary skin of ice
At low tide in the cove just north
Of Blue Hill Falls drapes and breaks
Over the ledges and sometimes submerged rocks
Like frosting on glazed doughnuts or hot cross buns;
It actually makes my mouth water.
I think of Lent and slowly coming spring.

CONTEMPLATION

> *My father, Harry D. Gideonse, was (to use the language he applied to others) a* ganz grosse Tier. *A College President (CUNY's Brooklyn College) and then Chancellor (New School for Social Research) for three quarters of his long professional life, he read voraciously, commented in print on a great deal of it, spoke with passion and high skill, worked in the cause of freedom, economics, and international affairs, and was not afraid of controversy. He was frequently called on by his peers in his many deliberative responsibilities to "let Harry wrap words around" their common understandings and conclusions. When he died twenty-five years ago I had a major opportunity to take stock of what he and my mother meant to me as I prepared remarks for their combined memorial services; they passed away within three weeks of each other. It would be two decades before I would have another go at what he meant to me. By that time I had become more experienced with metaphor even as I had had another third of my life to ruminate on his influences.*

Tendrils

The stairway to the second floor was narrow;
Despite the spindles on the right, it felt enclosed.
Its steep treads ended in a landing;
One stepped up to the right and doubled back
To gain access to the rest of the house.
But you couldn't climb those stairs without passing
The fair-sized room over the two-car garage
Lying, also up a step, at the stairway's head.

This was my father's study.

Bookshelves lined the walls from floor to ceiling
Save only for window spaces on three sides and
The closet door. The narrow space behind that door

Housed a four-drawer file,
A tidal flow of Barricini chocolates
In their many bags and boxes,
And, for several years, his mother's ashes
(Until *my* mother, with ceremony
And deliberate choice of place,
Dumped the old Tartar's remains in Gibraltar's strait).
My father's parakeets and Java birds hung out there,
And sometimes they flew free and tongued his
Cheeks and spectacles for salt –
"Pood-chee, pood-chee" he'd intone to egg them on.
When he was in this space the music flowed –
Beethoven, Strauss, Sousa, and Bach,
Rodgers, Gershwin, Lowe, Dvořák.
Two wingback chairs hovered heavy.
From the large table set before the window
Sprouted unkempt paper stacks,
But to he who'd grown them,
They were finely calibrated sets
Of archeologically defined – and precisely recalled – strata.
The chairs cradled the lanky, solid frame
Whose life force smoldered for ideas and words,
And the worlds those words defined,
Or shook,
Or split,
Or built,
Or canted ever slightly out of whack,
Or blew to smithereens.

A two-tiered table lamp held ashtrays, pencil jars and clips,
Spring-loaded sheers for clipping out the news, and a
        penknife.

On every vacant space and niche stood objet d'art,
Mementos of his travels round the globe.
Here as a brand-new teen is where I found and
Shared with younger brother, Marty,
The three fat picture folios of photographic nudes,
Visual preparation with considerable aesthetic style
For more corporeal adventures we each would have in years
        ahead.

This room was where my father spent the
Greatest portion of his day when he was home;
He'd read, and annotate, and write text on
Small white pads with #2 pencils always needing to be
        sharpened
(The penknife being the only tool I ever saw him use),
And do it in a script, if that not be dignifying it too much,
Only his secretary and, sometimes, my mother could decode.
In this room for fifteen years English Ovals could be found
(It was later he turned to pipes),
The slightly oblong boxes pleasing to the eye and hand,
Themselves a triumph of design,
The lidded top mating perfect to the base,
The folded over inner parchment wrap
Needing to be spread to reach the smokes inside.
He'd often forget he'd have one lit lying steady in his hand,
Smoke slowly curling by his index and middle fingers,
An ever longer growing twisted Cat-in-the-stovepipe-hat ash,
The tendril plume streaming straight up in the air
And then abruptly falling over itself like ribbon candy.
Those forgotten streams of smoke
Had dyed his fingers burnished gold.

On coming up the stairs
Music would foretell his presence when in residence, and
Just in case your ears were numb or otherwise engaged,
The swirling, lazy trails of exhaled smoke
Or just the pungent smell proclaimed him fully there.
This was his Sanctum Sanctorum wherein did dwell
The mighty power,
Mysterious,
Dark,
Precarious,
Portending hell.

We rarely entered when he was home,
As much because we knew he mustn't be disturbed –
Or certainly we dared not –
As there wasn't much with him we felt we shared
Save for the music, birds, and once a week our trips to
Pay a dollar on account against the balance of our latest loan
(Although I do recall a dollar flowing once the other way
The day I showed I'd met his challenge to commit
Lincoln's Gettysburg address to memory).

At arm's length, we were, it turns out, no less securely held.
We later – much later – learned, sometimes for good,
But sometimes staining, too,
His clasp entangled every sector of our lives,
Like smoke spilling from his study door
Seeping under all the thresholds of the house,
Reaching every floor.

> *For over forty years I had repeatedly told this story. It was only when I had become much more confident in my approaches to poetry that, telling the story once again, I would try my slowly developing skill in its service.*

MLK, Jr
May 6, 1964 First Parish Church, Brunswick, ME

Among the 1200 attending
There was at first silence,
Expectation, admiration
A collective holding of our breath.
The Baptist hero standing
A bare arm's length away
In this Congregational pulpit
Was knowable even from behind,
His shoulders braced,
Headed tilted up,
The surfaces of his robe beginning to whisper
As his body moved in time.
Rhythmical, resonant,
His voice complemented the deep mahogany tones
Of the polished lectern
Standing free of text or notes.
This pulpit had heard
Songs of intellect over time –
Jane Addams, Harriet Beecher Stowe,
Henry Wadsworth Longfellow,
Ralph Waldo Emerson, Henry Ward Beecher,
Eleanor Roosevelt –
And all the time that Martin spoke

His hands and fingers,
An even darker hue than the wood itself,
Ranged, taking readings of the molding,
The lectern's surfaces,
The pulpit rail,
Transcendent caresses
Running up and down the fluted edges
Drawing energy and inspiration
From wood oiled by the essence
Of twelve decades of principled ferment
Each touch summoning precious harmonies
To the deeply moral civil symphony
Issuing from his lips.

> *Joel White, the marine architect and boat builder, son of E.B., was something of a fixture in Brooklin, Maine. He was the kind of man who had an impact even on people who didn't know him well . . . like me, for example. I had perhaps half a dozen interactions with him beginning in the mid 70's when he graciously took a Saturday afternoon one July to fashion me a replacement stay which had half-parted in a way which suggested to him it had been struck by a projectile of some kind. There was something about the man that inspired comfort, calm, respect. I had driven down to the yard where* Wild Horses, *Joel's last boat, was standing waiting for her imminent launch. My youngest son was with me that evening. After we absorbed the scene, we returned to the car, but something drew me back to take a last long look alone before all light left the sky. The experience developed below was nearly a total surprise to me.*

Red Suspenders and *Wild Horses*

Maybe it was the red suspenders I was wearing
As I stood alone in deepest dusk of Center Harbor
Summer solstice night transfigured
By this last and largest of Joel White's wooden boats.
(I interchange my reds with rainbows,
But Joel's were almost signature;
I felt a slight embarrassment
At the near effrontery of my attire.)

Wild Horses stood before me . . .
And far, far above me . . .
And sweeping out to either side on left and right . . .
Near thirty tons of accelerating curves,

Excruciatingly fair surfaces,
Even in this near dark her harpoon line glinting gold,
Deceptive, one might say, plain,
Simplicity rising up to elegance.

My feet and the keel's massive bulb
Stood on the same level earth,
My eyes reaching upward to the waterline.
How supremely spare, I thought, the tube steel frame
To hold these heavy steeds of restless speed upright.
A line hanging from the bow
Ground-hitched her to the yard,
As if to keep the horses near
For all the doings two days hence
When first they feel the sea against their withers.

Twelve feet from the center line
And standing on the same plane,
A seventy-six foot boat
With ninety-plus foot mast is huge;
I felt like Mary Jane had spilled her magic sand
And made me small for some purpose
I could not begin to fathom.

The darker space and buildings grew,
The brighter the boat seemed to glow,
Her gleaming sides so smooth, so fair, so white
Above the sea green bottom paint,
She seemed to suck light from every distant source
And give it back from end to end.

The more she glowed, in fact,
The lighter yet she seemed to be,
A sense of straining to be free,
Her ground-hitch now transformed
Into a mast to moor
A dirigible wanting to float up,
To travel out beyond beyond,
For just a moment to think of flight,
To join Joel's spirit now sailing free,
Before fulfilling destiny
By running in the sea.

> *The years from 2001 through 2007 produced steadily mounting political discomfort and embarrassment as the Bush Administration displayed a level of incompetence seldom before seen in Washington. The Administration's practices, nationally and internationally, stood fundamentally at odds with everything America once believed about itself. When the President announced he would actually increase the number of troops serving in Iraq rather than the reverse, this was one result.*

Unheeded Meaning

Sixty-one years ago today,
Unable to comprehend
The horror of what had happened
Just three days before,
Our president and his generals
Failed to wave off the written plan,
And Superfortress "Bock's Car" left Tinian
To rain down on Nagasaki
What "Enola Gay" had
Delivered on Hiroshima.

Ten days ago we learned,
Despite the growing clamor
To reduce troop levels in Iraq,
Their numbers have instead increased
As canceled rotations out
Meant more troops could be sent
To Baghdad to cope with
The consequences of

Our failure to *have* a plan.

Yesterday a Bangor headline read
"Two dogs kill nine sheep, hurt ten";
Absent the llama and burro sentries,
The sheep were herded into mud,
Attacked relentlessly there
And others run by the dogs until
They dropped of exhaustion,
Their throats then rent
In senseless, useless slaughter.

Sixty-one years ago
Unable to comprehend
The horror of what had happened
Just three days before,
Our president and his generals
Failed to wave off the written plan,
And Superfortress "Bock's Car" left Tinian
To rain down on Nagasaki
What "Enola Gay" had
Dropped on Hiroshima.

> *His mother, grandmother, and grand aunt all decided to go shopping. Would I sit for Spencer William while they hit the mall? I'm fascinated by small children, but the chance not to have to tag along while they all undertook retail therapy only frosted my cake. And then this was the play, the sublime treat, I got to watch while they were gone.*

Spencer William's Hard Lovely Morn

He's three foot tall,
Two years of age,
And stands on the chair
He's dragged before the sink.
Small fingers hold
The plastic bottle cap
With purpose yet imperfect grasp,
The resolute untwisting,
Slow opening of the palm,
Then untwist again
And once off, then twisting back,
A bit more awkward and uncertain
Now the threads are free,
And succeeding all the same
Because I kept my cool
And didn't intercede
Although I thought
It might be past his skill.

Climbing down he grabs
Hold of the porcelain knob

Centered on the folding louver doors,
Takes risks on reaching in the opened space
As the forward movement
Of his body's inward reach
Threatens to close the door.
Still, reaching in among
The house-keeping handles
He finds the spindly cobweb wand
And uses it in mime; he vacuums
Back and forth on rugs and floors,
And underneath the bed,
With swiftness that isn't always
Mindful of the handle back
Which wavers to and fro
Beyond his view.

Back to the sink he
Leans forward at the waist,
Weight on his belly to keep
The chair from sliding out,
And reaches to the faucet lever
To push it back with care
And to the right --
Several times, in fact
(No risk of scalding
In this fellow's future!)
To fill a cup and pot,
And ladle back and forth
One to the other.
Picks up the liquid soap,
Presses down the button top
(Waste not want not at two?)

And plays at pouring soap
Into the half-filled sink.

Gets down and moves the chair
And takes it to the counter
Where the toaster oven sits,
Climbs up and lowers down the door
And slips the oven tray in on the rack,
Unhooks the hot pot shield
And slides it on the oven floor
And closes up the door,
And opens it again,
And plays it out once more.

Drags on the chair again
To where the CD player
Hangs beneath the cabinet door
And shows his knowledge
Of which switch works the light,
And which the player,
And which one again the light,
And then accepts with grace
My stepping in at youthful play
Which sent the CD tray way out
To risk his inadvertent torque
Or outright breaking off.

Finds once again the wand,
Resumes the vacuum play,
This time the living room.
Picks up Bert and Ernie's folding house,

Plays hard a quarter hour,
Then ambles over to where I've sat,
Climbs up and nestles down
And turns his face toward mine lips pursed
In silent ritual before rest,
And having had the kiss bestowed
Leans head and shoulder in,
Tucks knees into my lap,
And swiftly falls asleep.

> *I wrote this in celebration of poet Martin Steingesser's 70th birthday, and it was the poem I included in the 1958 Classbook for my fiftieth reunion at Amherst.*

70

Let me tell you about 70, Martin,
What I've learned in five months in the neighborhood . . .

It's a time when, in celebrations like this,
The strata of a fully lived life can come together,
Juxtapose themselves, touch, sidle up together
Like lazy, graceful swirls of metamorphosed rock.

It is a time when,
Relieved of the need to prove anything to anybody,
One can speak Socratic truths and take pride
In the occasional invitation to drink hemlock;
The prospect of eternity no longer holds the kind of threat
It did when we had most of life before us.

It is a time when love can return,
When the exquisite pleasure of two warm skins
Slip-sliding under winter covers
Can come back to a life too long without them,
When kisses showering all about turn out
Not to have been lost or confined in another time,
But only held in abeyance, dammed up, waiting for release.
It is a time when the truth of chemistry
In the life of love is deepened,

That while matches, flames, and fireworks
Are chemistry, to be sure,
So is the lichen's slow envelopment of stone
Or lime flowing in solution over time
Slowly making one column of stone
Where before there were two.

It is a time when gliding on the dimpled, eddying surface
Of a slow moving stream reminds one
That doubling back, reliving its delights,
Can be at least as thrilling as the
Whitewater rips of forty years ago.

So, it is a time of new and re-acquaintance,
Of rebirth belying images of dessication and decay
Others might ascribe to those only a year away
From an eighth decade's start.

Welcome to the neighborhood, new friend.

Hey, Mrs. Steingesser! Can Martin come out and play?

Parts of this poem were written over a half century ago as separate pieces. But they were elements of something larger which it took five decades to understand and express. And when they came together it grounded and secured a piece of a larger story.

Remembrance

You tumbled into my life
Without plan, worry, or regret,
No more than you displayed
That balmy night in Averill.
You walked me by the pasture,
Whistled the long lame Brownie over
Saying despite his hurt
You knew he still lived to ride,
And sliding your tight tan-jeaned self
Over the top rail of the fence
You grasped him round his neck,
Slid yourself aboard,
And rode away
Thundering hard
Into the dark
On muffled hooves,
Leaving me alone
To stand quiet
Heart in my mouth.
Long moments later you returned.

And then sometime after, you crossed the sea,
And when some months more, in spring,
You told me you'd come home,
Lilies of the valley
Became the bells of Bruges.

> *Just as Ringo Starr's "Photograph" took on a completely new and irreversible meaning once it was performed as part of the memorial concert for George Harrison, so this poem evolved into something completely new when the third stanza was added to memorialize Rufus Hellendale after he was taken from our community in the prime of his life.*

Come Spring . . .

Before being completely rebuilt,
Transformed to dine and cater to the well-to-do,
The picket fence of Blue Hill's Taylor/Clough/Wescott
       house
Each year framed a perfect case
Of dandelion lawn in spring –
As Barbara D. would say,
Millions and millions of yellow dandillions –
A molten flow of sunny fire before the door
So solid each year it could only light the
Darker corners of any soul who saw it.

Dandillion fire no longer flames the house,
A victim, no doubt, to a bent resident in me, too –
Let one scalawag dandillion
Invade the eclectic green around my home,
I'm out after it fork in hand.
Why, only weeks ago, in Bartlett's field
Across the road from me,
A singleton just off my path

140

Triggered neural semaphores
Down my spine and arm –
"Bend down, spear it, dig it out" –
Though nothing in my gait betrayed
The silent message sent and felt.

There's balance in all things, of course.
My friend Rufus would wryly pluck dandillions in full seed,
And moving slowly to where they were not,
He'd use his now stilled breath to launch the flyers
To light new flames brightening
Others' darkened corners in springs to come.

> *One of several dogs who have figured large in my past ten years, Arthur was a German Shepherd/Malamute mix. Near the end of his life I dog-sat for him many times as his parents traveled the country for family and art. When he'd come to visit Hogan he would be momentarily re-born, induced to puppy play and bursts of rollicking speed which briefly overcame his tendency to otherwise dodder.*

Lost Dog, Almost Gone

For Jacob, Melody and Dick

The call came sometime after eight.
Arthur'd gone out to pee, Mel said.
He'd had a pretty rugged night,
And now he'd not been seen for hours.
Would I come help and search
To find, perhaps, where he'd
Taken himself off to die?

Disappearing was nothing new for he whom
I sometimes thought of as "Spook;"
In my weekend and sometimes longer
Dog-sits at my home Arthur would be
Outdoors one moment,
There, right under foot,
The next just gone,
No sound or clue to tell you where.

Just as we'd thought since early Fall,
Arthur'd made it half way through winter,

Through fourteen recent sub-zero days,
But with the weather finally better
Perhaps he'd prepared himself to give it up,
His blue eyes ready to escape to
A wider sky's near perfect match.
In recent months he'd slipped
To skin and bones, his eyes sinking
Deep into his head, legs unsteady,
His feet slowly sliding outwards
With each step, sometimes even
When just standing still,
Until he'd lurch to find his balance
For yet one moment more.

The twenty minute drive was bright,
Stunning, really, after weeks of frigid air
And four storms that left the
Ridge fields white, swept,
And almost hurtful to the eyes.
The cold had broken, though.
I drove along a multi-hued morse code surface
Of finally-thawing country road,
The dits and dahs — white, brown,
Gray, black, and stainless steel where
Light reflects off the first wet in days —
Extend forward in random patterns
Parallel within the boundaries
Of plowed snow on either side.

Two black labs lie in a drive
Soaking sun, sucking up light
From the late January sky.

My own dog sits mournful by my side
As if he seems to know.
Turning down the drive
He gives a whimper, a barely audible whistle
Coming from deep, deep inside,
More apprehensive than impatient.

I let myself in the door always open to me,
Slip off my boots, hang up my coat, call out.
"You're here," I hear, and then
"I tried to call but you had left,
Arthur just came back,
Shaking, shivering,
Barely able to walk.
He's by the fire."

Covered by a throw, one ear moves
In greeting; I kneel and bend to whisper
The sweet nothings we both like,
Palm his ears.
He tongues my fingers in return,
But never raises his head.
His hind foot curls out
From under the throw, then pulls back.
It won't be long, that's clear,
Before he withdraws himself entirely.

* * * * * *

The time we would have spent in search

We spend on snowshoes on the river,
Relishing sculpted snow, ice fishing huts,
A pair of eagles.
And Hogan's boundless energy
Running, leaping, scrambling,
Nose poking eagerly into footprints,
Placed hours or maybe days before,
Nostril-down wolf-like trots,
Then shortened strides to cope with ice.

We pass the bold blunt rocky bluff
Where just last summer
Arthur'd climbed and drunk deeply of
A rockbound rain-replenished pool,
Enough, perhaps, to last 'til almost spring.

In time, I'll balance a stone
In his memory.

He's told us where.

I've learned I can never tell where or when an idea for a poem will grab me. I'd been shopping for years in Trade Winds, the locally owned and very skillfully operated supermarket, but it was the day my frequent encounters with the same shoppers suddenly made me realize that my strategies for attacking the task were really quite different from others'. I started paying attention to what had been right before my eyes all the time, and this was the result.

Cat's Cradle

I've been shopping for myself five years now
And for quite some time I've been aware I'm not the same
As many others who roll their carts to fill their larders
At one or another location on the peninsula.
A few, men mostly, march right in, no cart at all
Or even mini basket, stride right past the fruit,
Seize bread in one hand, a few more steps,
A package of meat, a dozen eggs, a carton of milk,
Rarely juice, it seems, and out they go.
Older couples seem paired up to pour over their lists,
Often staging Security Council debates over the merits
Of that cheese or this, Newman's sauce or someone else's,
Which cereal better balances fibre and flavor,
Whether that's the wine we liked or this other over here.
Young mothers, a child or two in tow,
Alternately amuse, or bribe, or scold, but generally prefer to
Hog the center aisle just past the reach of the toddler shopper
In the hopper of the cart.

Some follow plans carefully crafted in advance
But others come to play their moods; their carts sometimes
Leave no doubt which strategy's in play.
Some shoppers never miss an aisle,
Their pattern as methodically comprehensive
In their own packaged meadow as any herd of sheep;
Every aisle is traveled, every cul entered,
Every shelf scanned (or so it seems),
A weaver's approach, every aisle a warp, every shelf a woof
And when their shop is done their carts bulge at the seams,
Ready to spill forth like cornucopias at the checkout.

And then there's me, a little square or torn off note,
A script only I can read (and sometimes not!) so hastily was it
    done.
It sends me here and there, never anywhere else,
Zigzagging from vegetables to fruit
To meat, then dairy, fly to the beer, back to the soups
And then cookies, chips, and pop,
Whole sections of the store never looked in upon at all,
Systematic, too, my cat's cradle
Approach to marketing for myself.

> *My younger brother Martin died early January, 1998, and the next day an ice storm of epic proportions hammered the St. Lawrence River valley and a huge swath of central Maine. I first saw the damage three months later, and, as it happened, I did so on the drive back from the Cambridge memorial service for Marty. The respective feelings of grief became deeply intertwined.*
>
> *The poem holds a second meaning for me, now, because it was the first one where I had to fight in group to defend the images and the feelings against an arrogant attempt to impose a canon on me rather than a caring effort to help me improve my own work. A few years later that painful experience fueled my participation in a careful attempt to establish written parameters (included as an appendix to this volume) for a new writers' group seeking to help writers improve their craft and do so by avoiding hurt.*

April After Ice: Augusta to Belfast

Mile after mile, some blind, angered goddess
Has riffled the land with icy fingers
And dog-eared trees to mark
The roads, brooks, fields, and ponds
She could feel but not see.

Where her ice did not crimp the branches,
It swept off trees' crowns,
Dropping them this way and that
Beside the reaching stumps,
Great darts pointing skyward

To the source of their agony.
Many trunks are snapped, some clearly tortured,
Jagged-edged tank traps of warning
To any daemon thinking on another ice assault.

In settled stretches
The dead bodies of severed limbs stack up,
Sometimes six feet or more,
Butt ends to the road, racked for transport.

Here a birch mimes the shards
Of spent Independence Day salutes.
There another, even though it's April, a frozen arch
Still obeisant to the onslaught of three months before.
A large popple seems more vocal.
Its top lies broken, naked,
Arms reaching from the ground,
Cringing as in pain.
Some trees, maples mostly, leave good taste behind,
Their posteriors raised high, obscene,
A gesture of derision.
Others, split and peeled from nearly top to bottom,
Leave great tongues sticking from the forest in contempt . . .
Or maybe just to hang exhausted.

The worst damage by the roads
Has been removed from view,
Cut flush and shredded,
Turned to wood chips,
Like so much star dust on the forest floor.

In other places the land is newly bare.

Old stone walls, long lost, return to view.
Like fading coastal prints,
The dearth of trees evokes surprise.
It makes one think, but choose the context,
A clear cut can be merciful.

The forest holds its wake;
A thousand breaks flame orange in the setting sun,
The trunks like candles in the pre-green spring.

RAPTURE

> *Some initial encounters are a trickle, but a few are a flood.*

Savoring First Conversations

Beginning on the phone,
Then – as your internet profile forecast
Even before we met –
In the sun on a beach,
Our first conversations were like
Two cups of chopped onions
Lightly sautéed in extra virgin olive oil,
A handful of teaspoons of minced ginger root,
Two more of minced jalapeño,
Four cans of small black beans drained,
A couple more of tomatoes diced,
Fresh cut corn kernels from a half dozen ears,
A flower petal's throw of chopped pimento,
All folded into two-thirds of a cup
Of equal measures of light brown sugar and honey.
We added a teaspoon of thyme,
Simmered thirty minutes
In a covered iron skillet on the stove,
Then baked a half hour more,
And served it in a two-quart ceramic bowl
On its matching platter
To catch the almost
Certain overflow.

> *We all remember our very first kiss ever. But when a "first kiss" comes more than fifty years thereafter and feels so fresh it's like another brand new beginning all over again, then that seemed worth remarking on.*

First Kisses

Who ever loved that loved not at first sight?. - **Christoper Marlowe**

They were your initiative,
Two in number,
A gift to me,
Just like the hug you asked of me
The first time that we met
To walk Belfast's beaches.

Playful?
But of course!
Yet unlike any kiss I'd ever given
Or taken before,
They were a velvet hook,
A honeysuckle flute
Summoning the bee in me.

It was like sipping
From a tiny sensual teapot,
An offering of touch,
Like a toddler's hug,
Right there, bold,
Yet full-blown

In its innocence.

Three weeks later,
Remembering,
My insides leap up
Into the yawning well
Of my chest
Feeling all the world
Like I'm in the embrace
Of a shaggy lion lovey
From childhood.

> *A Nassau County Beach, a 'boy' and his dog, deep winter, howling snow . . .*

Lucky Dog

"No Dogs Allowed," the sign proclaims, and
"Beach Closed" just underneath
(One cancels out the other, right?);
I'd take the chance, leash law and all,
But not much of one it being
Doubtful any agent of the law
Will venture out this second day
Of winter wind and double digit snow
Dumping down upon New York.
So Hogan, straining at the leash as we
Climb the cross-dune stairs,
Will soon taste forbidden fruits
In the vast expanse of Lido Beach
Adrift in snow and ice to
Walk it disconnected, he and me.
Turns out we aren't first, not man nor beast,
Which makes it easier for me,
Still wracked by coughs of the deep weekend cold,
To walk in someone else's steps,
First over four feet of snowplow bank
And then through several three foot drifts
Sweeping right to left on the boardwalk
Across the sea oats of the dunes
Their plumes just barely peeping out
Of yesterday's two feet of snow.

My predecessor took a wayward track
To cross the dune which slows me down,
But not the dog who gaily hobbyhorses
His way through piled-up snow
Some of which swallows him whole
And then spits him out vertically,
Ears shaking, snout snorting in purest glee.
This storm isn't done; snow falls with new intensity.
The wind, while less than yesterday,
Still finds its way up sleeve and collar down.
We reach the beach wiped clean of snow
By rushing sweeps of sea, the remnants
Of chaotic waves pounding down just yards away.
A sandpiper runs water's edge,
Takes flight as the dog pursues
Who then stops sharply in his tracks
As waves taller than me by half
Just a hundred feet away
Tear a frightened NO! out of me,
A fear amended by the added thought that
A wet dog in the car driving to Manhattan
Was something devoutly to be avoided.

The sweeping waves
Have cut sharply into the beach
Leaving great pieces of layered mocha torte of sand,
Glazed icing hanging over
And sometimes crumbled on its plate.
An old tired snow fence, its slats long peeled away in disarray,
Its naked rusting posts bent this way and that by surf,
Still marches proudly, if somewhat drunk,

Out into the water in the general direction
Of where Ambrose Light used to be.

I didn't have to throw the stick he found;
The dog just grabs it up
At the tide line and turns
This improbable February day at the beach
Into a romp wholly of his own making,
Racing, breaking hind feet and fore
Through drifts initially seeming to promise
They'd suffice to hold him up!

After a time, we turn back.
He's at the ramp.
I call out Stay!
He does.
I retrace my path to where he waits
Reminded as I watch my steps of the riddle
Walking four feet in the morning,
Two at noon, and three at night,
My two feet and stick, two feet and stick,
A track symmetrical now that I return.

We stamp old snow and new
Off feet and boots.
Our hostess hears our walk report,
Retrieves a saying from our youth.
Lucky dog!, she says
Lucky dog, indeed, and
As important, lucky me!

> *Sara is the matriarch of a broad social group on Blue Hill peninsula which parties, saunas, potlucks, sails, and shares war stories of politics, art, and farming among other things. She spins, weaves, shepherds an extended family, takes annual trips to Greece where she keeps a second loom, but above all, she feels and lets it show!*

Mellow
    (for Sara)

I showed up to share the bounty
Of the deep good feelings
Spawned by a brand new
Affair de coeur of mine,
And over a glass of wine
On your brand new front door stoop
You were saying you were jealous of me,
And your old friend, too,
Now newly reconnected
To her high school sweetheart.

I asked you if you'd ever reached out to
A love seemingly lost in time,
Ever tried to track him down.
See where he might be,
Perhaps learn where you were, too.

You began to talk of Raul,
Whom you told nearly sixty years ago
You were far too young

To make that formal move called pinning
(But not too young, you said in retrospect,
To grasp and relish the tutoring
He freely gave to you).

"What do you think you know of him?" I asked.
You said for years he'd sent your mother cards
Each time your birthday came to pass.
(Well, I thought, taking silent notice!)
"He became an architect," you said,
"Lived in Miami,
"Close to Cuba,
"His father's home."

"Where's your computer?" I asked,
"If he's still alive,
We can find him,
But, the rest will be up to you."

We Googled;
Hey, we didn't even have to search!
There he was!

I turned and watched your face,
As the light in your eyes melted years,
Showed the shyness and joy of still being –
And being able to find – your seventeen,
An astounding transformation
Visible in your eyes, your cheeks,
Around your mouth,

A beaming back,
Tangoing once again
With the glow offering Raul
From the screen before us.

Quimby, now gone to his reward, was a very special critter, smallish, black, cute little face, little ears that hung down, seemed to walk by twisting himself into little curls, a very bushy tail almost always wagging, and a complete slut when it came to food – he'd follow – or stay – with anyone with a handout!. He belonged to a friend, Debrae, and I would care for him when she went to fairs or on long sails. Early on I had him for five weeks while she sailed to Nova Scotia. Quimby and I really bonded during that time, and it was my realization of what a difference a dog could make in the quality of my life that spurred me on to find Hogan. It was my perceptions about the changing qualities of my life and Quimby's role in creating awareness of them that led me to this poem.

Pancake
    (for Quimby)

Leading used to be important to me.
Command was almost second nature,
Intelligence a knife,
Or sometimes glue,
Or leverage to spring a rusted thread,
Or move a boulder from here to there,
And words were Archimedean levers
To move the world.
I liked to build, and
Summoned up inordinate stores
Of energy and will

That drove me on
To fuel a smoldering sense of quiet pride
That veiled, but oh so insecurely,
That sense of shame
And uncertain worth
So long ago instilled.

Of late I'd rather follow,
Allow my heart to lead instead of my head,
Absorbing silent,
Giving over of myself by being moved,
To lie quietly beneath the spangled coverlet of clear winter
    sky
And yet feel warm,
Thriving quiet in reverent honor
Of regularities I know inside
Yet don't quite understand.
I let this grown pup's licks of adoration
Around my nose
Compensate me for little breaths
Of love I send his way.

> This is the other side of 'Maple Syrup and Dandelions Gone to Seed' (p. 114). The poem interests me because it was written a second time in apparent unawareness I'd already undertaken it once. Two overlapping but still quite different poetical approaches to the same sequence of events. [sigh]

Dandelion Seed Puffs

The silky sepia tones of your skin,
Sensuous curve on curve,
So smooth, were my fingers tongues,
They would slide over you
As easily as an infant downs Junket.
When we held each other in late evening
And finally in early morning's quiet and warmth,
We were two dandelion puffs
One interweaving with the other,
And even when we'd briefly drift apart
No seed was out of place,
Our puffs still seeking to merge again,
And still again.

> *As one who used to be one, any policy maker would give his eye teeth to be able to achieve in those affected the kind of instantaneous understanding available to poets through the use of metaphor.*

First Fruit

Inclining lightly to my right
I turned your face toward me
And touched your yielding lips with mine.
An instant later I saw myself
Raising up my chin
Lest one ripe drop of liquid plum
Thus burst upon my mouth
Race down my neck untasted.

Glowworms

Summer heat hangs heavy,
Indolent,
An errant breeze just past our heads
Lightly fondling the gauzy curtain
Bent on straining last light out
Of the early evening air.
The well worn cotton sheets,
Having long since lost their cool,
Lie faintly humid,
Folded back and forth upon themselves,
The bubble tunnels they make rolling softly
Back and forth under our idling fingers.
Light leaks still faster from the
Fading day leaving behind
The faint persistent glow
Of body parts untouched by sun,
Fireflies signaling to connect,
Reminding us how passions just enflamed
Lie only banked to spark some later hour . . .

Or maybe even now?

> *There is much to be said for sustained periodic getaways to familiar surroundings. Over decades patterns emerge which themselves come to be essential parts of the processes of renewal, rebirth, and rejuvenation.*

Vacation

The each-year-repeated-week
Of work-related dreams has run its course.
The wind has angled on my face,
With the sun behind me seeming bright enough to
Penetrate my hat and hair and
Make my eyes glow inside out like a tiger's in the dark.
Rooster tails spray off the stays as the ketch heels
And dips its rail beneath the running wave.
I've had the chance to idle island beaches
Where the sea has left the usual surprises
On yards and yards of varied beaches –
Rockweed, some fresh, some dried, some foully rotting
Just waiting to stain your Docksiders,
A sea-tossed shaft of pine still
In its knotty erotic clasp now seen inside out,
Sand strewn blue with a hundred years of mussel shells,
A feather, a Mountain Dew bottle to recycle.
Back at the cottage there's a garden with greens to raid
And bush beans just starting to come.
The first brown and orange grins of
Black-eyed Susans beckon me to pick a
Bunch to grace the lunch scheduled for early afternoon.
Later, my brother lazes in the hammock on the porch
Revisiting Chingachcook and the Finger Lakes,

And in a not too distant tree,
A locust's whine escalates and then repeals,
Another way of gauging the yardarm's relation to the sun.
Glasses in hand we all gather up for dinner –
Lobsters steamed, sweet pickles,
Fresh picked greens and corn,
An *à la mode* pie of blueberries
The kids had picked that afternoon –
While the conversation at the table,
The classic hallmark of vacations at their best,
Explores in rich detail
What we all might just fix ourselves
For breakfast in the morning.

> *A storm can be threatening, dramatic, frightening – think Perfect Storm – but other connotations conjure up much more benign images albeit still sudden, powerful, all encompassing.*

Passing Storm

The storm pants through the open window, its sweet breath
Flowing past our heads, its flashing eyes illuminating
Droplets shaken from its shoulders onto ours.

We briefly stir. Your arm slips 'round me
To graze my cheek, entice my ear.
Thighs slide lightly clasping mine,
Shiny smooth as polished stone,
And just as cool.

The flashes lessen,
The storm abates.
It leaves us buoyant,
Languorous in repose,
Saturated,
Exquisite,
Quiet,
Calm.

> *This is a poem of moments in time – past, present, future – beginnings and endings, grieving, loving, contemplating, and even fun.*

Were I Solomon, This Would Be One of My Songs

Special moments these --
An into-the-wind lateral row
In a very choppy harbor
To a boat we would use to
Mull a family muddle
Sitting snug out of the wind
On the cockpit floor,
Backs to the cabin door;
A walk in the forest allowing us to claim
We'd finally toed at least one line
In our time together;
A card game on a log
In the middle of the woods,
One I would lose
But we would somehow
Both end up winning;
A visit to the fair, to horses, oxen,
Goats, chickens, rabbits, calves,
Boars, sows, prolific all,
And food, and drink, and food again;
A sail that turned instead into a

Canoe trip around Carney,
A landing, skipping stones,
A portage and picnic sauna,
Bathing naked amidst the clothed;
A moonbath cabin rocking gently
To the cries of gulls and gentle pings
Of halliards grazing metal masts;
An employee's half-price meal
Whose worth went way past fractions;
A peaceful sauna, slow, relaxed,
Repeated, and replete with quiet talk;
Tearful moments in the swing
Reminded by the beauty of the door, the pond,
The near blinding gold of rudbeckia
That Marty would never see
Or be amongst again;
The other grief, anticipated this time,
Of days like those recounted here
Eventually coming to a close,
Staying quietly alive, shared in memory,
Enriching us and others
Whom we touch and who touch us.

> *This volume began in gravitational balance and ends in synergy.*

An Electric Blanket Gone South

We lie within the chilly bed,
Your breasts molded to my back,
Unmistakable,
Though two layers of flannel intercede;
The tops of your thighs
Lightly frost the bottoms of mine.
The inside of your left calf
Edges over the outside left of mine.
I feel your cool sole slide and
Touch my metatarsals.

And then the bedclothes lose their chill.
The rise is slow,
Almost imperceptible,
Until one moment just past the next
The cold is neutralized and gone
Though warmth has not yet taken its place.

Comfort creeps upon us,
As, slowly, hearth and home are built,
Or children grow and go,
Or careers reach their peak and then,
Like gums, slightly recede.
The years together add stealth

And luscious patience to the repertoire.

We stir;
The comfort zone expands.
Warmth's slow contagion makes us turn
To nuzzle, kiss, caress,
And dance the dance four hundred months
Have given us time to hone.

Appendix

> *At one point in the journey this volume partially maps a number of us found ourselves experiencing real discomfort, and for a while we created an offshoot group. One outcome of that experience was the development of a formal prospectus which now, in its broad outlines, continues to inform the work of the several collections of writers currently active in the area. Against the possibility that others may have interest, the prospectus is included in this appendix.*

The Eggemoggin Writers' Collaborative Prospectus

Purpose

The Eggemoggin Writers' Collaborative (EWC) helps and supports writers in their craft by providing a continuing and demanding stimulus to encourage individual productive efforts. To achieve this purpose, individual members regularly present their work for analysis and evaluation by other members of the collaborative.

The work of the collaborative proceeds on the basis of mutual trust and respect and depends on the courage of its members both to publish [share] their work before one another and to share [offer] their candid and honest critiques of the work of other members. [Material brought to group is considered privileged. Respecting another's work, what is said here, stays here. If an author chooses to talk about his or her own work in other venues, however, any reactions of others shall be unidentified as to source. Confidentiality is fundamental to the Collaborative's success.]

The Collaborative limits itself to ten members to maintain the effectiveness and efficiency of the group. Additional members may be added as openings occur. A member's position will be forfeited, if he/she misses more than two consecutive meetings without reasonable cause.

Meetings

The EWC meets bi-weekly, currently every other Tuesday evening. Members who wish to socialize are asked to come at 6:30. Meetings begin promptly at 7 PM and conclude by 9 PM

Each meeting begins with brief announcements members may have of shared interest.

The bulk of each meeting is devoted to the reading and critique of member work.

Works presented must stand on their own without interpretation or explanation by the author.

From time to time, the collaborative may address its attention to a consensually agreed-upon already-published work.

The discussion of each work will begin with a short initial uninterrupted critique by each member. When all individuals have presented their individual critiques, respondents will then have an opportunity to further discuss the work.

Once discussion has been concluded, the author may choose to respond.

Each meeting is conducted by a Meeting Facilitator whose responsibilities are to encourage the active participation of each member, keep discussion focused on the author's work, and assist with the timely conclusion of each meeting.

Semi-annually as part of a regular meeting, the members review and, if necessary, re-work by consensus the purposes, procedures, and member roles within the collaborative.

Member Roles

In greater detail the roles of EWC members in meetings are delineated below.

Presenter

Alerts Meeting Facilitator of desire to present. If there are more presenters than can be handled at a given meeting, postponement to the next meeting may be negotiated among the presenters.

If the piece is part of a larger body of work, however, that should be indicated at the outset of the presentation. Authors will be asked to read from the text and to bring sufficient copies for each member to reference and take notes on.

Reads his or her work without advance explanation or substantive introduction. Poems are presented orally by the writer and then another group members is asked to volunteer to read the poem aloud a second time.

Listens silently until individual critiques and group discussion are completed as signaled by the Meeting Facilitator.

Presenters may – but are not obliged to – comment at the conclusion of the group discussion.

Respondent

Respondents listen carefully to the oral presentation.

Focus of individual critiques and any group discussion is to be on the work offered, and its purpose is to assist presenters in the improvement of their work.

Respondents are expected to be respectful of presenters and their work efforts and to be neither repetitive nor argumentative.

Respondents who wish to do so may provide authors with

additional written comments at the conclusion of the meeting or at a later time.

Host

Except as noted below, members are expected, each in their turn, to serve as hosts for the meetings. That includes opening their homes to members, and providing beverages and taste treats [generally, sugar and fat-laden snacks ;-) !] according to the season.

Meeting Facilitator

Normal expectation is that individual members will take turns serving in this role. Not everyone is uniquely suited to or prepared to undertake the role and some are quite effective in the role. (Individuals who are called upon more frequently to serve as facilitators may be excused from hosting responsibilities.) To perfect their facilitator skills, members may assume the facilitator role for several meetings in a row.

The facilitator agrees to take on the following responsibilities, and to lead a helpful, open-minded, discussion of the strengths and weaknesses of an author's work. In addition, the facilitator will guide the discussion, as needed, making certain that a supportive and safe environment for discussion is maintained.

All discussion shall focus solely on the work being presented. The facilitator is responsible for keeping speakers focused, not allowing side conversations, moving discussion along if it lags, maintaining order, and wrapping up the discussion when it has run its course.

Duties of Meeting Facilitator will include:

- Opening the meeting at 7 PM

- Calling for brief announcements

- Determining how many people wish to read

- Determining the type(s) and length of work to be read

- Selecting the order of readers

- Initiating rounds of responses to member work:

    Thanking the presenter (and second reader if a poem);
    Limiting individual critiques to approximately 2 to 3 minutes;
    Allowing each person present to make their initial critique before the floor opens to a broader discussion involving dialogue among the respondents;
    Keeping the discussion "on track" i.e., keeping it textually grounded and avoiding side conversations, digressions, repetitions, and argumentativeness;
    Maintaining order amongst participants;
    Watching for signs that someone has not had an opportunity to speak;
    Recognizing members and ceding them "the floor"; and
    Recognizing the author for possible responses at the conclusion of the group discussion.

- Bringing the meeting to a close at 9 PM after identifying the date of the next meeting, the meeting host, and the next Meeting Facilitator

September, 2000
Maureen Farr, Hendrik Gideonse, Caroline Scliffet, and Hank Whitsett.

Colophon*

The cover is set in Lithos, the title page and section headings in Lithograph. The main text is 12 pt Garamond, the introductory boxes 10 pt Garamond italic, and the Colophon 10 pt Garamond. Production was accomplished using lulu.com's capabilities. The stones balanced forever on the cover were raised for the briefest of moments – all that was necessary, really – in a cove on the northeast shore of Monhegan Island. (A rambunctious youngster knocked them over even as my partner, Sarah Margaret Longden, and I were climbing back to the walking trail.) The front cover and author's photos, the layout, and special lettering effects are by her. The back cover photo of the sauna with the only "cold-molded sauna door in Christendom" is by the author; the door's thru-handle formed from a u-shaped white cedar root was a gift of Rufus Hellendale – he may be gone from us but I still get to hang onto him coming and going! To Sarah Margaret I owe a debt it will be fun to continue to repay. She employed in my behalf her talents as a maker of books and her wide exposure to examples of book design possibilities; the page numbering graphic is hers and her instruction and Photoshop skills allowed me to craft the trademark symbol for the Gandalf Press. Without her contributions I would have achieved only a new pinnacle of the mundane.

And, finally, a few paragraphs on the journey which got me to this volume. I was trained as an historian and philosopher. Virtually all of my writing, with only a very rare and occasional exception (significantly, probably, a capacity to capture others' lives in obituary or eulogy) was exposition, argument, analysis, exhortation. It was systematic, grounded on data, as closely argued as I could manage, and necessarily linear. A policy analyst and formulator, an administrator in government and higher education, and an educational reformer, my colleagues will tell you I was known to have a hair shirt or two in my closet. (Alluded to in "70," years ago a philosopher friend gave me a tee shirt which read on the front "If we're not asking him to drink hemlock," and on the back "he's not doing his job!") I brought a huge amount of

---

* '... "publisher's inscription at the end of a book," from L. colophon, from Gk. kolophon "summit, final touch." '[Online Etymology Dictionary, © 2001 Douglas Harper] Subsequent research revealed the colophon, in point of fact, has been employed for whatever purposes writers or publishers desired. Q.E.D.

passion to my career; slowing down was only acceptable if it led to renewed energy, effort, and accomplishment. I retired in 1996 followed immediately thereafter by huge upheavals in my life as I lost my younger and only brother, my marriage of more than 30 years, and relocated back to Maine (where I had taken my first academic assignment at Bowdoin and had been returning for summer vacations for more than twenty years).

My writing always rested on two premises: it was important to leave tracks; and it is the only way to make one's thinking clear. I always trusted my writing intentionalities and in that period of emotional upheaval, I turned my attention accordingly. I knew a lot about writing *out* of passion; I knew nothing about expressing feelings per se, whatever they might be. In fact, I was full of a lot of potentially troublesome notions about writing which had to be set aside almost entirely if I were to learn to write in a new way. I'd have to learn to set aside shibboleths I had long carried around with me: Say it straight! To allude is to elude! Can the metaphor! Keep it cool! And so on.

In earlier years I *had* occasionally tried to write about my feelings. In retrospect those attempts were didactic, drivel, awful. The best that could be said about them was that I tried. I was not about to repeat that (although I would later revisit some of the early attempts, realize how bad they were in comparison to what I had thought to set out to do, and armed with that image, start over from scratch). And I was not afraid to ask for help; when I found out about local writers' groups I began to participate. My first (and very encouraging) surprise was that, even as I felt myself a complete neophyte as a writer of poetry, almost from the beginning I came to be viewed as a constructive critic. I was comfortable sticking to the text. While I would give my own reactions, I never thought to substitute my sense for the author's. And because I'd had a lot of editing experience myself, I knew something about the delicate balance between advice and . . . an avalanche!

Six individuals helped in the production of this volume by offering alternatives, advice, and support at a crucial time when I needed it, especially when I encountered platform instabilities in the actual production of the electronic text and format. My special thanks to Steve Brown, Maureen Farr, Ruth Howell, Laura Leader, Jay-Paul Thibault, and Mike Wolf.

Which seems like a perfect point to draw this colophon to a close. Designing, assembling, and editing the corpus has been a trip!   hdg

Main g

PORTLAND PUBLIC LIBRARY SYSTEM
5 MONUMENT SQUARE
PORTLAND, ME 04101

WITHDRAWN